MELAB®

SKILL PRACTICE

Practice Test

Questions for the MELAB®

We strongly recommend that students check with exam providers for up-to-date information regarding test content.

ISBN-13: 9781772452143

Version 6.6 April 2017

Published by
Complete Test Preparation Inc.
Victoria BC Canada

Or visit us on the web at http://www.test-preparation.ca
Printed in the USA

CONTENTS

Getting Started

ONGRATULATIONS! By deciding to take the MELAB®, you have taken the first step toward a great future! Of course, there is no point in taking this important examination unless you intend to do your best to earn the highest grade you possibly can. That means getting yourself organized and discovering the best approaches, methods and strategies to master the material. Yes, that will require real effort and dedication on your part but if you are willing to focus your energy and devote the study time necessary, before you know it you will be opening that letter of acceptance to the school of your dreams.

We know that taking on a new endeavour can be a little scary, and it is easy to feel unsure of where to begin. That's where we come in. This study guide is designed to help you improve your test-taking skills, show you a few tricks of the trade and increase both your competency and confidence.

What is on the MELAB®

The MELAB® has these sections: English grammar and Usage, Reading Comprehension, Essay, Vocabulary, Cloze, Listening Comprehension and an Oral Exam.

English – covers conversational grammar and English usage (30 questions).

Reading Comprehension – Four to five short passages are supplied with four to five multiple choice questions for each passage (20 - 30 questions).

Essay – write a short essay. Two topics are supplied.

Vocabulary – multiple choice vocabulary questions in two formats – vocabulary sentence completion, or meaning from context, and synonym substitution (25 – 30 questions).

Cloze – Fill in the blanks from a passage (15 – 20 questions).

Making a Study Schedule

To make your study time most productive you will need to develop a study plan. The purpose of the plan is to organize all the bits of pieces of information in such a way that you will not feel overwhelmed. Rome was not built in a day, and learning everything you will need to know to pass the MELAB® Exam is going to take time, too. Arranging the material you need to learn into manageable chunks is the best way to go. Each study session should make you feel as though you have succeeded in accomplishing your goal, and your goal is simply to learn what you planned to learn during that particular session. Try to organize the content in such a way that each study session builds upon previous ones. That way, you will retain the information, be better able to access it, and review the previous bits and pieces at the same time.

Take a look at the following table:

Exam Component	Rate from 1 to 5
Reading Comprehension	
Paragraph & Passage Comprehension	
Drawing Inferences & Conclusions	
English	
Spelling	
Grammar	
Punctuation	

Sentence Structure	
Essay Writing	
Cloze	
Vocabulary	

If you have areas in which you scored a five, congratulations! You will need just a very brief review to help you make the information easy to retrieve. Any area in which you scored a four is one that you need to review, but the review does not have to take long. For the most part, you already understand the material. Spending just a little time on it will remind you of what you know, and help you gain quick access to it.

Did you earn a three in one or more areas? Sharpen up the pencil, you have work to do! These sections will require a bit more time and determination. You have some understanding of the material, but you will need to focus on it to bring it front and center.

If you find yourself looking at a score below a three, you need to do some serious work. It is not going to be a matter of simply reviewing material to remind yourself of what you know, or spending a bit more time filling in the blanks between information that is at least somewhat familiar.

A zero, one or two means you really do not understand what you need to know, and these are the areas where you must concentrate most of your attention. You really need to work on these sections and make them your highest priority. Allocate the bulk of your study time to the areas in which you scored the lowest.

You are ready to create your study plan! If you have sufficient time, create a plan that spreads shorter study periods over more days. That way, you will stand a better chance of retaining the information. However, even a period of only five days can yield great results if you are organized. Let's say that Cloze is your downfall, and Punctuation and Essay

Writing are just a little bit better. The good news is that you got top scores in both reading comprehension and vocabulary, and your grasp of grammar is pretty good, as well. You will need to decide how much time to give each subject. Everyone's schedule will be different, depending upon how much available time there is. Here is an example of what you might decide:

Cloze: Study one hour every day, and review on last day

Punctuation: Study one hour for two days, then a half hour daily

Grammar: Review every second day

Essay Writing: Study and practice one hour on the first day then a half hour daily

Reading Comprehension: Review for a half hour every other day

Vocabulary: Review for a half hour every other day

It makes sense to focus your study time on those subjects where you need the most work but unless you create a visual chart for yourself, chances are good you will get confused in no time. First, write out what you need to study and how much time you want to devote to it. Next, consider how many days you have before the test. Plan to take time off from studying on the day before the exam is scheduled. On the last day before the test, you will not learn anything and will probably only confuse yourself. Besides, giving yourself a little break means you will feel fresher on the day of the test.

Make a table that includes slots for the number of days before the test and the number of hours you have available to study each day. We suggest working with half hour and one hour time slots; less than that means you will get set up to study and it will be time to quit, and more than an hour might result in mental fatigue.

Now you are ready to begin filling in the blanks. Give the most time to those subjects you need to study the most. It is also a good idea to assign your weakest subjects the most regular time slots. In fact, even just thirty minutes a day will help lock in the information you need. Of course, those subjects that you know like the back of your hand can be assigned the shortest blocks of time. You will note in the chart we have created that a half hour two or three times a week is all you will need for your strongest subjects.

y **Monday**	**Subject**	**Time**
Study	Vocabulary	1 hour
Study	Grammar & Usage	1 hour
	½ hour break	
Study	Cloze	1 hour
Review	Essay Writing	½ hour
Tuesday		
Study	Vocabulary	1 hour
Study	Grammar & Usage	½ hour
	½ hour break	
Study	Cloze	½ hour
Review	Essay Writing	½ hour
Review	General Review	½ hour
Study	Vocabulary	1 hour
Study	Grammar & Usage	½ hour
	½ hour break	
Study	Essay Writing	½ hour
Review	General Review	½ hour
Thursday		
Study	Vocabulary	½ hour
Study	Grammar & Usage	½ hour
Review	Cloze	½ hour
	½ hour break	
Review	Essay Writing	½ hour
Review	General Review	½ hour
Friday		
Review	Vocabulary	½ hour
Review	Grammar & Usage	½ hour
Review	Cloze	½ hour
	½ hour break	
Review	Essay Writing	½ hour
Review	Grammar & Usage	½ hour

TIPS FOR MAKING A SCHEDULE

Once you set a schedule that works, stick with it! Establish study sessions that are realistic. Blocking out study time that is too long or too short means you will be tempted to cheat. Instead, schedule study sessions that are reasonable and you will set yourself up for success!

Schedule breaks. Breaks are just as important as study time. Work out a rotation of studying and brief breaks that works for you.

Build up study time. If you find it hard to sit still and study for an hour at first, build up to it. Start with 20 minutes, and then take a break. Once you get used to 20-minute study sessions, increase the time to 30 minutes. Gradually work your way up to a full hour.

40 minutes to an hour is optimal. Studying for longer is unlikely to be productive. Studying for periods that are too short won't give you enough time to really learn anything.

PRACTICE TEST QUESTIONS SET 1

THE PRACTICE TEST PORTION PRESENTS QUESTIONS THAT ARE REPRESENTATIVE OF THE TYPE OF QUESTION YOU SHOULD EXPECT TO FIND ON THE MELAB®. However, they are not intended to match exactly what is on the MELAB®.

For the best results, take this Practice Test as if it were the real exam. Set aside time when you will not be disturbed, and a location that is quiet and free of distractions. Read the instructions carefully, read each question carefully, and answer to the best of your ability.

Use the bubble answer sheets provided. When you have completed the Practice Test, check your answer against the Answer Key and read the explanation provided.

VOCABULARY ANSWER SHEET

	A	B	C	D	E		A	B	C	D	E
1	○	○	○	○	○	21	○	○	○	○	○
2	○	○	○	○	○	22	○	○	○	○	○
3	○	○	○	○	○	23	○	○	○	○	○
4	○	○	○	○	○	24	○	○	○	○	○
5	○	○	○	○	○	25	○	○	○	○	○
6	○	○	○	○	○	26	○	○	○	○	○
7	○	○	○	○	○	27	○	○	○	○	○
8	○	○	○	○	○	28	○	○	○	○	○
9	○	○	○	○	○	29	○	○	○	○	○
10	○	○	○	○	○	30	○	○	○	○	○
11	○	○	○	○	○	31	○	○	○	○	○
12	○	○	○	○	○	32	○	○	○	○	○
13	○	○	○	○	○	33	○	○	○	○	○
14	○	○	○	○	○	34	○	○	○	○	○
15	○	○	○	○	○	35	○	○	○	○	○
16	○	○	○	○	○	36	○	○	○	○	○
17	○	○	○	○	○	37	○	○	○	○	○
18	○	○	○	○	○	38	○	○	○	○	○
19	○	○	○	○	○	39	○	○	○	○	○
20	○	○	○	○	○	40	○	○	○	○	○

READING COMPREHENSION ANSWER SHEET

	A	B	C	D	E		A	B	C	D	E
1	○	○	○	○	○	21	○	○	○	○	○
2	○	○	○	○	○	22	○	○	○	○	○
3	○	○	○	○	○	23	○	○	○	○	○
4	○	○	○	○	○	24	○	○	○	○	○
5	○	○	○	○	○	25	○	○	○	○	○
6	○	○	○	○	○	26	○	○	○	○	○
7	○	○	○	○	○	27	○	○	○	○	○
8	○	○	○	○	○	28	○	○	○	○	○
9	○	○	○	○	○	29	○	○	○	○	○
10	○	○	○	○	○	30	○	○	○	○	○
11	○	○	○	○	○						
12	○	○	○	○	○						
13	○	○	○	○	○						
14	○	○	○	○	○						
15	○	○	○	○	○						
16	○	○	○	○	○						
17	○	○	○	○	○						
18	○	○	○	○	○						
19	○	○	○	○	○						
20	○	○	○	○	○						

English Grammar Answer Key

	A	B	C	D	E		A	B	C	D	E
1	○	○	○	○	○	21	○	○	○	○	○
2	○	○	○	○	○	22	○	○	○	○	○
3	○	○	○	○	○	23	○	○	○	○	○
4	○	○	○	○	○	24	○	○	○	○	○
5	○	○	○	○	○	25	○	○	○	○	○
6	○	○	○	○	○	26	○	○	○	○	○
7	○	○	○	○	○	27	○	○	○	○	○
8	○	○	○	○	○	28	○	○	○	○	○
9	○	○	○	○	○	29	○	○	○	○	○
10	○	○	○	○	○	30	○	○	○	○	○
11	○	○	○	○	○	31	○	○	○	○	○
12	○	○	○	○	○	32	○	○	○	○	○
13	○	○	○	○	○	33	○	○	○	○	○
14	○	○	○	○	○	34	○	○	○	○	○
15	○	○	○	○	○	35	○	○	○	○	○
16	○	○	○	○	○	36	○	○	○	○	○
17	○	○	○	○	○	37	○	○	○	○	○
18	○	○	○	○	○	38	○	○	○	○	○
19	○	○	○	○	○	39	○	○	○	○	○
20	○	○	○	○	○	40	○	○	○	○	○

CLOZE ANSWER SHEET

	A	B	C	D
1	◯	◯	◯	◯
2	◯	◯	◯	◯
3	◯	◯	◯	◯
4	◯	◯	◯	◯
5	◯	◯	◯	◯
6	◯	◯	◯	◯
7	◯	◯	◯	◯
8	◯	◯	◯	◯
9	◯	◯	◯	◯
10	◯	◯	◯	◯
11	◯	◯	◯	◯
12	◯	◯	◯	◯
13	◯	◯	◯	◯
14	◯	◯	◯	◯
15	◯	◯	◯	◯
16	◯	◯	◯	◯
17	◯	◯	◯	◯
18	◯	◯	◯	◯
19	◯	◯	◯	◯
20	◯	◯	◯	◯

PART 1 - VOCABULARY

1. She performed the gymnastics and stretches so well! I have never seen anyone so <u>nimble</u>.

    a. Awkward

    b. Agile

    c. Quick

    d. Taut

2. Are there any more <u>queries</u>? We have already had so many questions today.

    a. Questions

    b. Commands

    c. Obfuscations

    d. Paradoxes

3. The tide was in this morning but now it is starting to <u>recede</u>.

    a. Go out

    b. Flow

    c. Swell

    d. Come in

4. I don't think that will make it any better - it is just going to <u>aggravate</u> the situation.

    a. Worsen

    b. Precipitate

    c. Elongate

    d. None of the above

5. I didn't think this was her first appearance, but it is her <u>debut</u>.

    a. Exit

    b. Introduction

    c. Curtain Call

    d. Resignation

6. His library is enormous. I didn't realize he was such a <u>bibliophile</u>.

    a. Book lover

    b. Audiophile

    c. Bibliophobe

    d. Audiophobe

7. I thought they were being very discreet, but they were, in fact, very <u>flagrant</u>.

    a. Obvious

    b. Secretive

    c. Hidden

    d. Subtle

8. He goes for coffee everyday. It is his <u>habitual</u> start to the day.

    a. Customary

    b. Rare

    c. Unchanging

    d. Unusual

9. She is just crazy about Britney Spears. She <u>idolizes</u> her a little too much I think.

    a. Fears

    b. Worships

    c. Rejects

    d. Refutes

10. She has been to some very dangerous places. She is an <u>intrepid</u> explorer.

    a. Brave

    b. Timid

    c. Timorous

    d. Cowardly

11. He wasn't especially generous. All the servings were very <u>judicious</u>.

    a. Abundant

    b. Careful

    c. Sparing

    d. Careless

12. She presented a pretty good case up to now, but the latest evidence tends to <u>negate</u> everything he has said.

    a. Disagree

    b. Reinforce

    c. Improve

    d. None of the above

13. It is boring and I would rather not go, but the ceremony is <u>obligatory</u>.

    a. Mandatory

    b. Optional

    c. Adaptable

    d. None of the above.

14. We used that operating system 20 years ago, now it is <u>obsolete</u>.

    a. Functional

    b. Disused

    c. Obese

    d. None of the Above.

15. His bad manners really <u>rankle</u> me.

    a. Annoy

    b. Obfuscate

    c. Enliven

    d. None of the above.

16. We don't want to hear the whole thing. Just the <u>salient</u> facts please.

    a. Irrelevant

    b. Erroneous

    c. Relevant

    d. Trivial

17. She works in a cubicle answering the phone all day. Her doctor says she is too <u>sedentary</u>.

    a. Inactive

    b. Active

    c. Morbid

    d. None of the Above.

18. I don't know why he is being so nice. I am sure he has an <u>ulterior</u> motive.

    a. Inferior

    b. Additional

    c. Simplistic

    d. Unfortunate

19. We cannot reveal the source. It was posted by <u>anonymous</u>.

    a. Unidentified

    b. Author

    c. Someone

    d. Nobody

20. I have never seen anyone so rude. His behavior was <u>atrocious</u>.

    a. Monstrous

    b. Perfect

    c. Unwarranted

    d. Suspicious

21. He lived on the streets from a very early age and still is a _____.

    a. Sally

    b. Rue

    c. Pliable

    d. Waif

22. His jokes were very crude and he is very rude. I always thought he was very _____.

    a. Opaque

    b. Obnoxious

    c. Proficient

    d. Morbid

23. She is very thoughtful and _____ today.

    a. Pensive

    b. Paternal

    c. Passe

    d. Parochial

24. I am finally out of debt! I paid off all of my _____.

    a. Debtors

    b. Defendants

    c. Accounts Receivable

    d. Creditors

25. I love listening to his speeches. He has a gift for _____.

    a. Oratory

    b. Irony

    c. Jargon

    d. None of the above

26. The repair really isn't working. Those parts you re-placed are _____.

    a. Despondent

    b. Illusive

    c. Deficient

    d. Granular

27. Her inheritance was a good size and included many _____.

    a. Heirlooms

    b. Perchance

    c. Cynical

    d. Lateral

28. He hadn't shaved and his hair was messy. I said he couldn't go looking so _____.

    a. Uncouth

    b. Unkempt

    c. Unerring

    d. Tawdry

29. When Joe broke his _____ in a skiing accident, his entire leg was in a cast.

    a. Ankle

    b. Humerus

    c. Wrist

    d. Femur

30. Alan had to learn the _____ system of numbering when his family moved to Great Britain.

    a. American

    b. Decimal

    c. Metric

    d. Fingers and toes

31. After Lisa's aunt had her tenth child, Lisa found that she had more than twenty _____.

    a. Uncles

    b. Friends

    c. Stepsisters

    d. Cousins

32. Although the boy had taken many trips by plane, this was his first flight in a _____.

    a. Helicopter

    b. Kite

    c. Train

    d. Subway car

33. George is very serious about _____, and recently joined the American Scholastic Association.

    a. Schoolwork

    b. Cooking

    c. Travelling

    d. Athletics

34. She was a rabid Red Sox fan, attending every game, and demonstrating her _____ by cheering more loudly than anyone else.

    a. Knowledge

    b. Boredom

    c. Commitment

    d. Enthusiasm

35. When Craig's dog was struck by a car, he rushed his pet to the _____.

    a. Emergency room

    b. Doctor

    c. Veterinarian

    d. Podiatrist

36. After she received her influenza vaccination, Nan thought that she was _____ to the common cold.

    a. Immune

    b. Susceptible

    c. Vulnerable

    d. At risk

37. Paul's rose bushes were being destroyed by Japanese beetles, so he invested in a good _____.

    a. Fungicide

    b. Fertilizer

    c. Sprinkler

    d. Pesticide

38. The last time that the crops failed, the entire nation experienced months of _____.

    a. Famine

    b. Harvest

    c. Plenitude

    d. Disease

39. Because of a pituitary dysfunction, Karl lacked the necessary _____ to grow as tall as his father.

    a. Glands

    b. Hormones

    c. Vitamins

    d. Testosterone

40. Because of its colorful fall _____, the maple is my favorite tree.

    a. Growth

    b. Branches

    c. Greenery

    d. Foliage

SECTION II - READING COMPREHENSION.

Directions: The following questions are based on a number of reading passages. Each passage is followed by a series of questions. Read each passage carefully, and then answer the questions based on it. You may reread the passage as often as you wish. When you have finished answering the questions based on one passage, go right on to the next passage. Choose the best answer based on the information given and implied.

Questions 1 – 4 refer to the following passage.

Passage 1 - Infectious Disease

An infectious disease is a clinically evident illness resulting from the presence of pathogenic agents, such as viruses, bacteria, fungi, protozoa, multi cellular parasites, and unusual proteins known as prions. Infectious pathologies are also called communicable diseases or transmissible diseases, due to their potential of transmission from one person or species to another by a replicating agent (as opposed to a toxin).

Transmission of an infectious disease can occur in many different ways. Physical contact, liquids, food, body fluids, contaminated objects, and airborne inhalation can all transmit infecting agents.

Transmissible diseases that occur through contact with an ill person, or objects touched by them, are especially infective, and are sometimes referred to as contagious diseases. Communicable diseases that require a more specialized route of infection, such as through blood or needle transmission, or sexual transmission, are usually not regarded as contagious.

The term infectivity describes the ability of an organism to enter, survive and multiply in the host, while the infectiousness of a disease indicates the comparative ease with which the disease is transmitted. An infection however, is not synonymous with an infectious disease, as an infection may not cause important clinical symptoms. [8]

1. What can we infer from the first paragraph in this passage?

a. Sickness from a toxin can be easily transmitted from one person to another.

b. Sickness from an infectious disease can be easily transmitted from one person to another.

c. Few sicknesses are transmitted from one person to another.

d. Infectious diseases are easily treated.

2. What are two other names for infections' pathologies?

a. Communicable diseases or transmissible diseases

b. Communicable diseases or terminal diseases

c. Transmissible diseases or preventable diseases

d. Communicative diseases or unstable diseases

3. What does infectivity describe?

a. The inability of an organism to multiply in the host

b. The inability of an organism to reproduce

c. The ability of an organism to enter, survive and multiply in the host

d. The ability of an organism to reproduce in the host

4. How do we know an infection is not synonymous with an infectious disease?

a. Because an infectious disease destroys infections with enough time.

b. Because an infection may not cause important clinical symptoms or impair host function.

c. We do not. The two are synonymous.

d. Because an infection is too fatal to be an infectious disease.

Questions 5 – 8 refer to the following passage.

Passage 2 - Viruses

A virus (from the Latin virus meaning toxin or poison) is a small infectious agent that can replicate only inside the living cells of other organisms. Most viruses are too small to be seen directly with a microscope. Viruses infect all types of organisms, from animals and plants to bacteria and single-celled organisms.

Unlike prions and viroids, viruses consist of two or three parts: all viruses have genes made from either DNA or RNA, all have a protein coat that protects these genes, and some have an envelope of fat that surrounds them when they are outside a cell. (Viroids do not have a protein coat and prions contain no RNA or DNA.) Viruses vary from simple to very complex structures. Most viruses are about one hundred times smaller than an average bacterium. The origins of viruses in the evolutionary history of life are unclear: some may have evolved from plasmids—pieces of DNA that can move between cells—while others may have evolved from bacteria.

Viruses spread in many ways; plant viruses are often transmitted from plant to plant by insects that feed on sap, such as aphids, while animal viruses can be carried by blood-sucking insects. These disease-bearing organisms are known as vectors. Influenza viruses are spread by coughing and sneezing. HIV is one of several viruses transmitted through sexual contact and by exposure to infected blood. Viruses can infect only a limited range of host cells called the "host range". This can be broad as when a virus is capable of infecting many species or narrow. [9]

5. What can we infer from the first paragraph in this selection?

a. A virus is the same as bacterium

b. A person with excellent vision can see a virus with the naked eye

c. A virus cannot be seen with the naked eye

d. Not all viruses are dangerous

6. What types of organisms do viruses infect?

a. Only plants and humans

b. Only animals and humans

c. Only disease-prone humans

d. All types of organisms

7. How many parts do prions and viroids consist of?

a. Two

b. Three

c. Either less than two or more than three

d. Less than two

8. What is one common virus spread by coughing and sneezing?

   a. AIDS

   b. Influenza

   c. Herpes

   d. Tuberculosis

Questions 9 – 11 refer to the following passage.

Passage 3 – Clouds

The first stage of a thunderstorm is the cumulus stage, or developing stage. In this stage, masses of moisture are lifted upwards into the atmosphere. The trigger for this lift can be insulation heating the ground producing thermals, areas where two winds converge, forcing air upwards, or where winds blow over terrain of increasing elevation. Moisture in the air rapidly cools into liquid drops of water, which appears as cumulus clouds.

As the water vapor condenses into liquid, latent heat is released which warms the air, causing it to become less dense than the surrounding dry air. The warm air rises in an updraft through the process of convection (hence the term convective precipitation). This creates a low-pressure zone beneath the forming thunderstorm. In a typical thunderstorm, approximately 5×10^8 kg of water vapor is lifted, and the amount of energy released when this condenses is about equal to the energy used by a city of 100,000 in a month. [10]

9. The cumulus stage of a thunderstorm is the

    a. The last stage of the storm

    b. The middle stage of the storm formation

    c. The beginning of the thunderstorm

    d. The period after the thunderstorm has ended

10. One of the ways the air is warmed is

    a. Air moving downwards, which will creates a high-pressure zone

    b. Air cooling and becoming less dense, causing it to rise

    c. Moisture moving downward toward the earth

    d. Heat created by water vapor condensing into liquid

11. Identify the correct sequence of events

    a. Warm air rises, water droplets condense, creating more heat, and the air rises farther.

    b. Warm air rises and cools, water droplets condense, causing low pressure.

    c. Warm air rises and collects water vapor, the water vapor condenses as the air rises, which creates heat, and causes the air to rise farther.

    d. None of the above.

Questions 12 – 14 refer to the following passage.

Passage 4 – US Weather Service

The United States National Weather Service classifies thunderstorms as severe when they reach a predetermined level. Usually, this means the storm is strong enough to inflict wind or hail damage. In most of the United States, a storm is considered severe if winds reach over 50 knots (58 mph or 93 km/hr), hail is ¾ inch (2 cm) diameter or larger, or if meteorologists report funnel clouds or tornadoes. In the Central Region of the United States National Weather Service, the hail threshold for a severe thunderstorm is 1 inch (2.5 cm) in diameter. Though a funnel cloud or tornado indicates the presence of a severe thunderstorm, the various meteorological agencies would issue a tornado warning rather than a severe thunderstorm warning in this case.

Meteorologists in Canada define a severe thunderstorm as either having tornadoes, wind gusts of 90 km/hr or greater, hail 2 centimeters in diameter or greater, rainfall more than 50 millimeters in 1 hour, or 75 millimeters in 3 hours.

Severe thunderstorms can develop from any type of thunderstorm. [10]

12. What is the purpose of this passage?

a. Explaining when a thunderstorm turns into a tornado

b. Explaining who issues storm warnings, and when these warnings should be issued

c. Explaining when meteorologists consider a thunderstorm severe

d. None of the above

13. It is possible to infer from this passage that

a. Different areas and countries have different criteria for determining a severe storm

b. Thunderstorms can include lightning and tornadoes, as well as violent winds and large hail

c. If someone spots both a thunderstorm and a tornado, meteorological agencies will immediately issue a severe storm warning

d. Canada has a much different alert system for severe storms, with criteria that are far less

14. What would the Central Region of the United States National Weather Service do if hail was 2.7 cm in diameter?

a. Not issue a severe thunderstorm warning.

b. Issue a tornado warning.

c. Issue a severe thunderstorm warning.

d. Sleet must also accompany the hail before the Weather Service will issue a storm warning.

Questions 15 – 18 refer to the following passage.

Passage 5 – Clouds

A cloud is a visible mass of droplets or frozen crystals floating in the atmosphere above the surface of the Earth or other planetary bodies. Another type of cloud is a mass of material in space, attracted by gravity, called interstellar clouds and nebulae. The branch of meteorology which studies clouds is called nephrology. When we are speaking of Earth clouds, water vapor is usually the condensing substance, which forms small droplets or ice crystal. These crystals are typically 0.01 mm in diameter. Dense, deep clouds reflect most light, so they appear white, at least from the top. Cloud droplets scatter light very efficiently, so the further into a cloud light travels, the weaker it gets. This accounts for the gray or dark appearance at the base of large clouds. Thin clouds may appear to have acquired the color of their environment or background. [10]

15. What are clouds made of?

a. Water droplets.

b. Ice crystals.

c. Ice crystals and water droplets.

d. Clouds on Earth are made of ice crystals and water droplets.

16. The main idea of this passage is

a. Condensation occurs in clouds, having an intense effect on the weather on the surface of the earth.

b. Atmospheric gases are responsible for the gray color of clouds just before a severe storm happens.

c. A cloud is a visible mass of droplets or frozen crystals floating in the atmosphere above the surface of the Earth or other planetary body.

d. Clouds reflect light in varying amounts and degrees, depending on the size and concentration of the water droplets.

17. The branch of meteorology that studies clouds is called

a. Convection

b. Thermal meteorology

c. Nephology

d. Nephelometry

18. Why are clouds white on top and grey on the bottom?

a. Because water droplets inside the cloud do not reflect light, it appears white, and the further into the cloud the light travels, the less light is reflected making the bottom appear dark.

b. Because water droplets outside the cloud reflect light, it appears dark, and the further into the cloud the light travels, the more light is reflected making the bottom appear white.

c. Because water droplets inside the cloud reflects light, making it appear white, and the further into the cloud the light travels, the more light is reflected making the bottom appear dark.

d. None of the above.

Questions 19 - 22 refer to the following recipe.

Chocolate Chip Cookies

3/4 cup sugar
3/4 cup packed brown sugar
1 cup butter, softened
2 large eggs, beaten
1 teaspoon vanilla extract
2 1/4 cups all-purpose flour
1 teaspoon baking soda
3/4 teaspoon salt
2 cups semisweet chocolate chips

If desired, 1 cup chopped pecans, or chopped walnuts.
Preheat oven to 375 degrees.

Mix sugar, brown sugar, butter, vanilla and eggs in a large bowl. Stir in flour, baking soda, and salt. The dough will be very stiff.

Stir in chocolate chips by hand with a sturdy wooden

spoon. Add the pecans, or other nuts, if desired. Stir until the chocolate chips and nuts are evenly dispersed.

Drop dough by rounded tablespoonfuls 2 inches apart onto a cookie sheet.

Bake 8 to 10 minutes or until light brown. Cookies may look underdone, but they will finish cooking after you take them out of the oven.

19. What is the correct order for adding these ingredients?

      a. Brown sugar, baking soda, chocolate chips

      b. Baking soda, brown sugar, chocolate chips

      c. Chocolate chips, baking soda, brown sugar

      d. Baking soda, chocolate chips, brown sugar

20. What does sturdy mean?

      a. Long

      b. Strong

      c. Short

      d. Wide

21. What does disperse mean?

      a. Scatter

      b. To form a ball

      c. To stir

      d. To beat

22. When can you stop stirring the nuts?

a. When the cookies are cooked.

b. When the nuts are evenly distributed.

c. As soon as the nuts are added.

d. After the chocolate chips are added.

Questions 23 – 25 refer to the following passage.

Passage 7 – Caterpillars

Butterfly larvae, or caterpillars, eat enormous quantities of leaves and spend practically all their time in search of food. Although most caterpillars are herbivorous, a few species eat other insects. Some larvae form mutual associations with ants. They communicate with ants using vibrations transmitted through the soil, as well as with chemical signals. The ants provide some degree of protection to the larvae and they in turn gather honeydew secretions. [11]

23. What do most larvae spend their time looking for?

a. Leaves

b. Insects

c. Leaves and insects

d. Honeydew secretions

24. What benefit do larvae get from association with ants?

a. They do not receive any benefit

b. Ants give them protection

c. Ants give them food

d. Ants give them honeydew secretions

25. Do ants or larvae benefit most from association?

   a. Ants benefit most.

   b. Larvae benefit most.

   c. Both benefit the same.

   d. Neither benefits.

Questions 26 – 30 refer to the following passage.

Passage 8 – Navy Seals

The United States Navy's Sea, Air and Land Teams, commonly known as Navy SEALs, are the U.S. Navy's principal special operations force, and a part of the Naval Special Warfare Command (NSWC) as well as the maritime component of the United States Special Operations Command (USSOCOM).

The unit's acronym ("SEAL") comes from their capacity to operate at sea, in the air, and on land – but it is their ability to work underwater that separates SEALs from most other military units in the world. Navy SEALs are trained and have been deployed in a wide variety of missions, including direct action and special reconnaissance operations, unconventional warfare, foreign internal defence, hostage rescue, counter-terrorism and other missions. All SEALs are members of either the United States Navy or the United States Coast Guard.

In the early morning of 2 May 2011 local time, a team of 40 CIA-led Navy SEALs completed an operation to kill Osama bin Laden in Abbottabad, Pakistan about 35 miles (56 km) from Islamabad, the country's capital. The Navy SEALs were part of the Naval Special Warfare Development Group, previously called "Team 6". President Barack Obama later confirmed the death of bin Laden. The unprecedented media coverage raised the public profile of the SEAL community, particularly the counter-terrorism specialists commonly known as SEAL Team 6. [12]

26. Are Navy SEALs part of USSOCOM?

    a. Yes

    b. No

    c. Only for special operations

    d. No, they are part of the US Navy

27. What separates Navy SEALs from other military units?

    a. Belonging to NSWC

    b. Direct action and special reconnaissance operations

    c. Working underwater

    d. Working for other military units in the world

28. What other military organizations do SEALs belong to?

    a. The US Navy

    b. The Coast Guard

    c. The US Army

    d. The Navy and the Coast Guard

29. What other organization participated in the Bin Laden raid?

    a. The CIA

    b. The US Military

    c. Counter-terrorism specialists

    d. None of the above

30. What is the new name for Team 6?

a. They were always called Team 6

b. The counter-terrorism specialists

c. The Naval Special Warfare Development Group

d. None of the above

PART III – ENGLISH GRAMMAR AND USAGE

1. Choose the sentence with the correct usage.

a. Even with an speed limit sign clearly posted, an inattentive driver may drive too fast.

b. Even with a speed limit sign clearly posted, a inattentive driver may drive too fast.

c. Even with an speed limit sign clearly posted, a inattentive driver may drive too fast.

d. Even with a speed limit sign clearly posted, an inattentive driver may drive too fast.

2. Choose the sentence with the correct usage.

a. Except for the roses, she did not accept John's frequent gifts.

b. Accept for the roses, she did not except John's frequent gifts.

c. Accept for the roses, she did not accept John's frequent gifts.

d. Except for the roses, she did not except John's frequent gifts.

3. Choose the sentence with the correct usage.

a. Although he continued to advise me, I no longer took his advice.

b. Although he continued to advice me, I no longer took his advise.

c. Although he continued to advise me, I no longer took his advise.

d. Although he continued to advice me, I no longer took his advise.

4. Choose the sentence with the correct usage.

a. To adopt to the climate, we had to adopt a different style of clothing.

b. To adapt to the climate, we had to adapt a different style of clothing.

c. To adapt to the climate, we had to adopt a different style of clothing.

d. To adapt to the climate, we had to adapt a different style of clothing.

5. Choose the sentence with the correct usage.

a. When he's between friends, Robert seems confident, but between you and me, he is really very shy.

b. When he's among friends, Robert seems confident, but among you and me, he is really very shy.

c. When he's between friends, Robert seems confident, but among you and me, he is really very shy.

d. When he's among friends, Robert seems confident, but between you and me, he is really very shy.

6. Choose the sentence with the correct usage.

a. I will be finished at ten in the morning, and will be arriving at home at about 6:30.

b. I will be finished at about ten in the morning, and will be arriving at home at 6:30.

c. I will be finished at about ten in the morning, and will be arriving at home at about 6:30.

d. I will be finished at ten in the morning, and will be arriving at home at 6:30.

7. Choose the sentence with the correct usage.

a. Beside the red curtains and pillows, there was a red rug beside the couch.

b. Besides the red curtains and pillows, there was a red rug beside the couch.

c. Besides the red curtains and pillows, there was a red rug besides the couch.

d. Beside the red curtains and pillows, there was a red rug besides the couch.

8. Choose the sentence with the correct usage.

a. Although John can swim very well, the lifeguard may not allow him to swim in the pool.

b. Although John may swim very well, the lifeguard may not allow him to swim in the pool.

c. Although John can swim very well, the lifeguard cannot allow him to swim in the pool.

d. Although John may swim very well, the lifeguard may not allow him to swim in the pool.

9. Choose the sentence with the correct usage.

a. Her continuous absences caused a continual disruption at the office.

b. Her continual absences caused a continuous disruption at the office.

c. Her continual absences caused a continual disruption at the office.

d. Her continuous absences caused a continuous disruption at the office.

10. Choose the sentence with the correct usage.

a. During the famine, the Irish people had to emigrate to other countries; many of them immigrated to the United States.

b. During the famine, the Irish people had to immigrate to other countries; many of them immigrated to the United States.

c. During the famine, the Irish people had to emigrate to other countries; many of them emigrated to the United States.

d. During the famine, the Irish people had to immigrate to other countries; many of them emigrated to the United States.

11. Choose the sentence with the correct usage.

a. His home was farther than we expected; farther, the roads were very bad.

b. His home was farther than we expected; further, the roads were very bad.

c. His home was further than we expected; further, the roads were very bad.

d. His home was further than we expected; farther, the roads were very bad.

For Each Of The Sentences Below Choose The Correct Word To Replace The Underlined Word Or Phrase.

12. We'll go to the beach <u>in</u> our vacation.

   a. On

   b. At

   c. From

   d. None of the above

13. We'll go to the beach during the <u>summer vocations</u>.

   a. Summer vacation

   b. Summer's vacation

   c. Summer vocation

   d. Summers vacation

14. Richard is the <u>tallest</u> of the two boys.

   a. Tall

   b. Taller

   c. Taller than

   d. None of the above

15. We must help the needy and <u>poors</u>.

   a. The poor

   b. Poor

   c. The poors

   d. None of the above

Fill In The Blanks.

16. Our _____ to America by sea was not very comfortable.

    a. Journey

    b. Voyage

    c. Travel

    d. None of the above

17. I do not want to _____ a friend like you.

    a. Lose

    b. Loose

    c. Lost

    d. None of the above

18. This pain killer will _____ your pain.

    a. Lesson

    b. Lessen

    c. Lesen

    d. Leson

Select The Correct Version Of The Sentences

19. Why did Mr. Simpson deny to help you?

    a. Why did Mr. Simpson refuse to help you?

    b. Why did Mr. Simpson resist to help you?

    c. Why did Mr. Simpson not accept to help you?

    d. The sentence is correct.

20. She is the <u>most cleverest</u> girl in the class.

    a. She is the most clever girl in the class.

    b. She is the cleverest girl in the class.

    c. She is the most cleverer girl in the class.

    d. The sentence is correct.

21. Choose the sentence with the correct grammar.

    a. The dog took the stuffed toy to his master's empty chair.

    b. The dog brang the stuffed toy to his master's empty chair.

    c. The dog brought the stuffed toy to his master's empty chair.

    d. The dog taken the stuffed toy to his master's empty chair.

22. Choose the sentence with the correct grammar.

    a. Until you take the overdue books to the library, you can't take any new ones home.

    b. Until you take the overdue books to the library, you can't bring any new ones home.

    c. Until you bring the overdue books to the library, you can't take any new ones home.

    d. Until you take the overdue books to the library, you can't take any new ones home.

23. Choose the sentence with the correct grammar.

    a. Newer cars use fewer gasoline and produce fewer emissions.

    b. Newer cars use less gasoline and produce less emissions.

    c. Newer cars use less gasoline and produce fewer emissions.

    d. Newer cars fewer less gasoline and produce less emissions.

24. Choose the sentence with the correct grammar.

a. His doctor suggested that he eat less snacks and do fewer lounging on the couch.

b. His doctor suggested that he eat fewer snacks and do less lounging on the couch.

c. His doctor suggested that he eat less snacks and do less lounging on the couch.

d. His doctor suggested that he eat fewer snacks and do fewer lounging on the couch.

25. Choose the sentence with the correct grammar.

a. However, I believe that he didn't really try that hard.

b. However I believe that he didn't really try that hard.

c. However; I believe that he didn't really try that hard.

d. However: I believe that he didn't really try that hard.

26. Choose the sentence with the correct grammar.

a. There was however, very little difference between the two.

b. There was, however very little difference between the two.

c. There was; however, very little difference between the two.

d. There was, however, very little difference between the two.

27. Choose the sentence with the correct grammar.

a. Don would never have thought of that book, but you could have reminded him.

b. Don would never of thought of that book, but you could have reminded him.

c. Don would never have thought of that book, but you could of have reminded him.

d. Don would never of thought of that book, but you could of reminded him.

28. Choose the sentence with the correct grammar.

a. The mother would not of punished her daughter if she could have avoided it.

b. The mother would not have punished her daughter if she could of avoided it.

c. The mother would not of punished her daughter if she could of avoided it.

d. The mother would not have punished her daughter if she could have avoided it.

29. Although Joe is tall for his age, his brother Elliot is _____ of the two.

a. The tallest

b. More tallest

c. The tall

d. The taller

30. When Kiss came to town, all of the tickets _____ before I could buy one.

a. Will be sold out

b. Had been sold out

c. Were being sold out

d. Was sold out

31. The rules of most sports _____ more complicated than we often realize.

    a. Are

    b. Is

    c. Was

    d. Has been

32. Neither of the Wright Brothers _____ that they would be successful with their flying machine.

    a. Have any doubts

    b. Has any doubts

    c. Had any doubts

    d. Will have any doubts

33. The Titanic _____ mere days into its maiden voyage.

    a. Has already sunk

    b. Will already sunk

    c. Already sank

    d. Sank

34. _____ won first place in the Western Division?

    a. Who

    b. Whom

    c. Which

    d. What

35. There are now several ways to listen to music, including radio, CDs, and Mp3 files _____ you can download onto an Mp3 player.

    a. On which

    b. Who

    c. Whom

    d. Which

PART IV – CLOZE

Passage 1 - Foxes

In the wild, foxes ___1___ live for up to 10 years, but most foxes only live for 2 to 3 years due to hunting, road accidents and diseases. Foxes are generally smaller than other canines ___2___ wolves, jackals, and domestic dogs.

> Reynards or male foxes, weigh, on average, around 5.9 kilograms (13 lbs.) and vixens, or female foxes, weigh ___3___, at around 5.2 kilograms (11.5 lbs.). Fox-like features typically include a distinctive muzzle (a "fox face") and bushy tail. Other physical characteristics vary according to habitat. For example, the fennec fox, and other species of fox ___4___ to life in the desert, have large ears ___5___ short fur, whereas the Arctic fox has tiny ears and thick, insulating fur. ___6___ example is the red fox, which has a tail ___7___ white markings. Litter sizes can vary greatly according to species and environment – the Arctic Fox, for example, has an ___8___ litter of four to five, with up to eleven in a litter.[13]

1.

    a. can

    b. may

2.

    a. or

    b. such as

3.

    a. more

    b. less

4.

    a. adapted

    b. adopted

5.

    a. and

    b. or

6.

    a. another

    b. more

7.

    a. and

    b. with

8.

    a. average

    b. size

Passage 2 - Alice in Wonderland – Chapter 1 – Down the Rabbit Hole.

Alice was beginning to get very tired of sitting by her sister on the river bank, and of having nothing to ___9___: once or twice she had ___10___ into the book her sister was reading, but it had no pictures or conversations ___11___ it, 'and what is the use of a book,' thought Alice 'without pictures or conversation?'

So she was considering in her own mind (as well as she could, for the hot day made her ___12___ very sleepy and stupid), whether the pleasure of making a daisy-chain would be worth the trouble of getting up and ___13___ the daisies, when suddenly a White Rabbit with pink eyes ran close by her.

There was nothing so VERY remarkable in that; nor did Alice think it so VERY much out of the way to ___14___ the Rabbit say to itself, 'Oh dear! Oh dear! I shall be late!' (when she thought it over ___15___, it occurred to her that she ought to have wondered at this, but ___16___ it all seemed quite natural); but when the Rabbit actually took ___17___ watch out of its waistcoat-pocket, and looked ___18___ it, and then hurried on, Alice started to her feet, for it flashed across her mind that she had never before seen a rabbit with either a waistcoat-pocket, or a watch to take out of it, and burning with curiosity, she ran across the field after it, and fortunately was just in time to see it pop down a large rabbit-hole under the hedge.[14]

9.

    a. does

    b. do

10.

    a. peeped

    b. read

11.

    a. on

    b. in

12.

    a. feel

    b. felt

13.

    a. picking

    b. pick

14.

    a. hear

    b. heard

15.

    a. afterwards

    b. before

16.

      a. at the time

      b. on the time

17.

      a. a

      b. an

18.

      a. to

      b. at

PRACTICE TEST 1 - ANSWER KEY

Part I - Vocabulary

1. B
Nimble: Quick and light in movement or action.

2. A
Queries: Questions or inquiries.

3. A
Recede: To move back, to move away.

4. A
Aggravate: to make worse, or more severe; to render less tolerable or less excusable; to make more offensive; to enhance; to intensify.

5. B
Debut: a performer's first-time performance to the public.

6. A
Bibliophile: one who loves books.

7. A
Flagrant: obvious and offensive, blatant, scandalous.

8. A
Habitual: Behaving in a regular manner, as a habit.

9. B
Idolize: To make an idol of, or to worship as an idol.

10. A
Intrepid: Fearless; bold; brave.

11. B
Judicious: Having, or characterized by, good judgment or sound thinking.

12. A
Negate: To deny the existence, evidence, or truth of; to contradict.

13. A
Obligatory: Imposing obligation, morally or legally; binding: an obligatory promise.

14. B
Obsolete: no longer in use; gone into disuse; disused or neglected.

15. A
Rankle: To cause irritation or deep bitterness.

16. C
Salient: Worthy of note; pertinent or relevant.

17. A
Sedentary: Not moving; relatively still; staying in the vicinity.

18. B
Ulterior: beyond what is obvious or evident.

19. A
Anonymous: Of unknown name; whose name is withheld.

20. A
Atrocious: very bad; abominable or disgusting

21. D
Waif: a wanderer; a castaway; a stray; a homeless child.

22. B
Obnoxious: very annoying, offensive, odious or contemptible.

23. A
Pensive: having the appearance of deep, often melancholic, thinking.

24. D
Creditors: A person to whom a debt is owed.

25. A
Oratory: the art of public speaking, especially in a formal, expressive, or forceful manner.

26. C
Deficient: lacking something essential;

27. A
Heirloom: A valued possession that has been passed down through the generations.

28. B
Unkempt: dishevelled; untidy; dirty; not kept up.

29. D
Femur: A thighbone.

30. C
Metric: of or relating to the metric system of measurement.

31. D
Cousins: The son or daughter of a person's uncle or aunt; a first cousin.

32. A
Helicopter: An aircraft that is borne along by one or more sets of long rotating blades which allow it to hover, move in any direction including reverse, or land; and having a smaller set of blades on its tail that stabilize the aircraft.

33. B
Schoolwork

34. D
Enthusiasm: Intensity of feeling; excited interest or eagerness.

35. C
Veterinarian: A medical doctor who treats animals.

36. A
Immune: Exempt; not subject to.

37. D
Pesticide: A substance, usually synthetic although sometimes biological, used to kill or contain the activities of pests.

38. A
Famine: extreme shortage of food in a region.

39. B
Hormones: Any substance produced by one tissue and conveyed by the bloodstream to another to effect physiological activity.

40. D
Foliage: The leaves of plants.[4]

PART II – READING COMPREHENSION

1. B
We can infer from this passage that sickness from an infectious disease can be easily transmitted from one person to another.

From the passage, "Infectious pathologies are also called communicable diseases or transmissible diseases, due to their potential of transmission from one person or species to another by a replicating agent (as opposed to a toxin)."

2. A
Two other names for infectious pathologies are communicable diseases and transmissible diseases.

From the passage, "Infectious pathologies are also called communicable diseases or transmissible diseases, due to their potential of transmission from one person or species to another by a replicating agent (as opposed to a toxin)."

3. C
Infectivity describes the ability of an organism to enter, survive and multiply in the host. This is taken directly from the passage, and is a definition type question.

Definition type questions can be answered quickly and easily by scanning the passage for the word you are asked to define.

"Infectivity" is an unusual word, so it is quick and easy to scan the passage looking for this word.

4. B
We know an infection is not synonymous with an infectious disease because an infection may not cause important clinical symptoms or impair host function.

5. C
We can infer from the passage that, a virus is too small to be seen with the naked eye. Clearly, if they are too small to be seen with a microscope, then they are too small to be seen with the naked eye.

6. D
Viruses infect all types of organisms. This is taken directly from the passage, "Viruses infect all types of organisms, from animals and plants to bacteria and single-celled organisms."

7. C
The passage does not say exactly how many parts prions and viroids consist of. It does say, "Unlike prions and viroids, viruses consist of two or three parts ..." so we can infer they consist of either less than two or more than three parts.

8. B
A common virus spread by coughing and sneezing is influenza.

9. C
The cumulus stage of a thunderstorm is the beginning of the thunderstorm.

This is taken directly from the passage, "The first stage of a thunderstorm is the cumulus, or developing stage."

10. D
The passage lists four ways that air is heated. One of the ways is, heat created by water vapor condensing into liquid.

11. A
The sequence of events can be taken from these sentences:

As the moisture carried by the [1] air currents rises, it rapidly cools into liquid drops of water, which appear as cumulus clouds. As the water vapor condenses into liquid, it [2] releases heat, which warms the air. This in turn causes the air to become less dense than the surrounding dry air and [3] rise further.

12. C
The purpose of this text is to explain when meteorologists consider a thunderstorm severe.

The main idea is the first sentence, "The United States National Weather Service classifies thunderstorms as severe when they reach a predetermined level." After the first sentence, the passage explains and elaborates on this idea. Everything is this passage is related to this idea, and there are no other major ideas in this passage that are central to the whole passage.

13. A
From this passage, we can infer that different areas and countries have different criteria for determining a severe storm.

From the passage we can see that most of the US has a criteria of, winds over 50 knots (58 mph or 93 km/hr), and hail ¾ inch (2 cm). For the Central US, hail must be 1 inch (2.5 cm) in diameter. In Canada, winds must be 90 km/hr or greater, hail 2 centimeters in diameter or greater, and rainfall more than 50 millimeters in 1 hour, or 75 millimeters in 3 hours.

Choice D is incorrect because the Canadian system is the

same for hail, 2 centimeters in diameter.

14. C
With hail above the minimum size of 2.5 cm. diameter, the Central Region of the United States National Weather Service would issue a severe thunderstorm warning.

15. D
Clouds in space are made of different materials attracted by gravity. Clouds on Earth are made of water droplets or ice crystals.

Choice D is the best answer. Notice also that choice D is the most specific.

16. C
The main idea is the first sentence of the passage; a cloud is a visible mass of droplets or frozen crystals floating in the atmosphere above the surface of the Earth or other planetary body.

The main idea is very often the first sentence of the paragraph.

17. C
Nephology, which is the study of cloud physics.

18. C
This question asks about the process, and gives options that can be confirmed or eliminated easily.

From the passage, "Dense, deep clouds reflect most light, so they appear white, at least from the top. Cloud droplets scatter light very efficiently, so the farther into a cloud light travels, the weaker it gets. This accounts for the gray or dark appearance at the base of large clouds."

We can eliminate choice A, since water droplets inside the cloud do not reflect light is false.

We can eliminate choice B, since, water droplets outside the cloud reflect light, it appears dark, is false.

Choice C is correct.

19. A

The correct order of ingredients is brown sugar, baking soda and chocolate chips.

20. B

Sturdy: strong, solid in structure or person. In context, Stir in chocolate chips by hand with a *sturdy* wooden spoon.

21. A

Disperse: to scatter in different directions or break up. In context, Stir until the chocolate chips and nuts are evenly *dispersed*.

22. B

You can stop stirring the nuts when they are evenly distributed. From the passage, "Stir until the chocolate chips and nuts are evenly dispersed."

23. A

Larvae spend most of their time in search of food and their food is leaves.

24. B

From the passage, the ants provide some degree of protection

25. C

The association is mutual so both benefit.

26. A

Navy SEALs are the maritime component of the United States Special Operations Command (USSOCOM).

27. C

Working underwater separates SEALs from other military units. This is taken directly from the passage.

28. D

SEALs also belong to the Navy and the Coast Guard.

29. A

The CIA also participated. From the passage, the raid was conducted by a "team of 40 *CIA-led* Navy SEALS."

30. C

From the passage, "The Navy SEALs were part of the Naval Special Warfare Development Group, previously called 'Team 6'."

PART III ENGLISH ANSWER KEY

1. D

The article "a" come before a noun that begins with a consonant, while "an" comes before a noun that begins with a vowel.

2. A

"Except" means to exclude something. "Accept" means to receive something, or to agree to an idea.

3. A

"Advise" is a verb that means to offer advice, which is a noun.

4. C

"Adapt" means to change or accommodate. "Adopt" means to accept, embrace, or to assume responsibility or ownership for something or someone.

5. D

"Among" is used with more than two items, while "between" is limited to two items.

6. D

"At" refers to a specific time or location, while "about" is approximate.

7. B

"Beside" means next to, and "besides" means in addition to.

8. A

"Can" is used when describing ability or capability. "May" is a request or the granting of permission.

9. B

"Continuous" means a time period without interruption, or ongoing. "Continual" is used for actions that are frequent and repetitive, or that continue almost without interruption.

10. A

"Emigrate" means to leave one's country, usually to immigrate to another country to live.

11. A

"Farther" is reserved for physical distance, and "further" is used for figurative distance, or to mean "in addition."

12. A

"On" is the preposition that is used with vacations and holidays.

13. D

The correct choice is "summer vacation." A "vocation" is a job or occupation.

14. B

"Taller" is used when comparing two things. "Tallest" is used when comparing more than two things.

15. B

"The poor" refers to a group of indigent people; however, in this sentence it is unnecessary to repeat "the."

16. B

"Travel" is a verb meaning to go from one place to another. A "journey" is a noun that refers to the travel event. A "voyage" is a journey by sea.

17. A

"Lose" is a verb meaning to misplace something or to fail at a competition. "Loose" is an adjective meaning untied or able to move freely.

18. B

"Lessen" means to reduce in size or intensity. "Lesson"

refers to a formal time period in which particular information is taught or learned.

19. A
"Deny" means to reject or disagree with the truth of something. "Refuse" means to decline to do or accept something.

20. B
"Cleverest" is the superlative form, and means the most clever.

21. A
Whether to use "bring" or "take" depends on location. Something coming toward the subject's location is brought. Something going away from the subject's location is taken.

22. C
Whether to use "bring" or "take" depends on location. Something coming toward the subject's location is brought. Something going away from the subject's location is taken.

23. C
"Fewer" is used with countable nouns and "less" is used with uncountable nouns.

24. B
"Fewer" is used with countable nouns and "less" is used with uncountable nouns.

25. A
"However" is bracketed with a comma after it at the beginning of a sentence.

26. D
"However" is bracketed with a comma before and after it within a sentence.

27. A
The third conditional is used for talking about an unreal

situation (a situation that did not happen) in the past. For example, "If I had studied harder, [if clause] I would have passed the exam" [main clause]. This has the same meaning as, "I failed the exam, because I didn't study hard enough."

28. D
The third conditional is used for talking about an unreal situation (a situation that did not happen) in the past. For example, "If I had studied harder, [if clause] I would have passed the exam" [main clause]. This has the same meaning as, "I failed the exam, because I didn't study hard enough."

29. D
When comparing two items, use "the taller." When comparing more than two items, use "the tallest."

30. B
The past perfect form is used to describe an event that occurred in the past and prior to another event.

31. A
The subject is "rules" so the present tense plural form, "are," is used to agree with "realize."

32. C
The simple past tense, "had," is correct because it refers to completed action in the past.

33. D
The simple past tense, "sank," is correct because it refers to completed action in the past.

34. A
"Who" is correct because the question uses an active construction. "To whom was first place given?" is passive construction.

35. D
"Which" is correct, because the files are objects and not people.

PART IV – CLOZE

1. A
"Can" expresses ability and "may" expresses permission.

2. B
Here the sentence is giving examples, so "such as" is correct.

3. B
Female foxes weigh less.

4. A
"Adapt" means to change or accommodate. "Adopt" means to accept, embrace, or to assume responsibility or ownership for something or someone.

5. A
"And" is correct.

6. A
Use "another" because "example" is singular.

7. B
The red fox has a tail **with** white markings.

8. A
Average is correct.

9. B
The correct form is "nothing to do."

10. A
To "peep" is to look briefly.

11. B
The preposition "in" is correct. To say, "on the book," means on the outside of the book.

12. A
The present tense, "feel" is correct.

13. A
The present progressive, "picking" is correct in this sentence, to match, "getting up."

14. A
The present tense "hear" is correct.

15. A
When she thought it over "afterwards" is correct.

16. A
"At the time" refers to a precise time.

17. A
"Watch" begins with a consonant, so "a" is correct.

18. B
"Look at" is correct.

PRACTICE TEST QUESTIONS SET II

THE PRACTICE TEST PORTION PRESENTS QUESTIONS THAT ARE REPRESENTATIVE OF THE TYPE OF QUESTION YOU SHOULD EXPECT TO FIND ON THE MELAB®. However, they are not intended to match exactly what is on the MELAB®.

For the best results, take this Practice Test as if it were the real exam. Set aside time when you will not be disturbed, and a location that is quiet and free of distractions. Read the instructions carefully, read each question carefully, and answer to the best of your ability.

Use the bubble answer sheets provided. When you have completed the Practice Test, check your answer against the Answer Key and read the explanation provided.

VOCABULARY ANSWER SHEET

	A	B	C	D	E		A	B	C	D	E
1	○	○	○	○	○	21	○	○	○	○	○
2	○	○	○	○	○	22	○	○	○	○	○
3	○	○	○	○	○	23	○	○	○	○	○
4	○	○	○	○	○	24	○	○	○	○	○
5	○	○	○	○	○	25	○	○	○	○	○
6	○	○	○	○	○	26	○	○	○	○	○
7	○	○	○	○	○	27	○	○	○	○	○
8	○	○	○	○	○	28	○	○	○	○	○
9	○	○	○	○	○	29	○	○	○	○	○
10	○	○	○	○	○	30	○	○	○	○	○
11	○	○	○	○	○	31	○	○	○	○	○
12	○	○	○	○	○	32	○	○	○	○	○
13	○	○	○	○	○	33	○	○	○	○	○
14	○	○	○	○	○	34	○	○	○	○	○
15	○	○	○	○	○	35	○	○	○	○	○
16	○	○	○	○	○	36	○	○	○	○	○
17	○	○	○	○	○	37	○	○	○	○	○
18	○	○	○	○	○	38	○	○	○	○	○
19	○	○	○	○	○	39	○	○	○	○	○
20	○	○	○	○	○	40	○	○	○	○	○

READING COMPREHENSION ANSWER SHEET

	A	B	C	D	E		A	B	C	D	E
1	○	○	○	○	○	21	○	○	○	○	○
2	○	○	○	○	○	22	○	○	○	○	○
3	○	○	○	○	○	23	○	○	○	○	○
4	○	○	○	○	○	24	○	○	○	○	○
5	○	○	○	○	○	25	○	○	○	○	○
6	○	○	○	○	○	26	○	○	○	○	○
7	○	○	○	○	○	27	○	○	○	○	○
8	○	○	○	○	○	28	○	○	○	○	○
9	○	○	○	○	○	29	○	○	○	○	○
10	○	○	○	○	○	30	○	○	○	○	○
11	○	○	○	○	○						
12	○	○	○	○	○						
13	○	○	○	○	○						
14	○	○	○	○	○						
15	○	○	○	○	○						
16	○	○	○	○	○						
17	○	○	○	○	○						
18	○	○	○	○	○						
19	○	○	○	○	○						
20	○	○	○	○	○						

English Grammar Part 1 Answer Key

	A	B	C	D	E		A	B	C	D	E
1	○	○	○	○	○	21	○	○	○	○	○
2	○	○	○	○	○	22	○	○	○	○	○
3	○	○	○	○	○	23	○	○	○	○	○
4	○	○	○	○	○	24	○	○	○	○	○
5	○	○	○	○	○	25	○	○	○	○	○
6	○	○	○	○	○	26	○	○	○	○	○
7	○	○	○	○	○	27	○	○	○	○	○
8	○	○	○	○	○	28	○	○	○	○	○
9	○	○	○	○	○	29	○	○	○	○	○
10	○	○	○	○	○	30	○	○	○	○	○
11	○	○	○	○	○	31	○	○	○	○	○
12	○	○	○	○	○	32	○	○	○	○	○
13	○	○	○	○	○	33	○	○	○	○	○
14	○	○	○	○	○	34	○	○	○	○	○
15	○	○	○	○	○	35	○	○	○	○	○
16	○	○	○	○	○	36	○	○	○	○	○
17	○	○	○	○	○	37	○	○	○	○	○
18	○	○	○	○	○	38	○	○	○	○	○
19	○	○	○	○	○	39	○	○	○	○	○
20	○	○	○	○	○	40	○	○	○	○	○

English Grammar Part II - Answer Key

```
      A  B  C  D
 1   ○  ○  ○  ○
 2   ○  ○  ○  ○
 3   ○  ○  ○  ○
 4   ○  ○  ○  ○
 5   ○  ○  ○  ○
 6   ○  ○  ○  ○
 7   ○  ○  ○  ○
 8   ○  ○  ○  ○
 9   ○  ○  ○  ○
10   ○  ○  ○  ○
11   ○  ○  ○  ○
12   ○  ○  ○  ○
13   ○  ○  ○  ○
14   ○  ○  ○  ○
15   ○  ○  ○  ○
16   ○  ○  ○  ○
17   ○  ○  ○  ○
18   ○  ○  ○  ○
19   ○  ○  ○  ○
20   ○  ○  ○  ○
```

PART 1 – READING AND LANGUAGE ARTS

VOCABULARY

1. I still don't know exactly. That isn't <u>conclusive</u> evidence.

    a. Undeterred

    b. Unrelenting

    c. Unfortunate

    d. Definitive

2. His investment scheme <u>duped</u> many serious investors, who lost money.

    a. Helped

    b. Vindicated

    c. Fooled

    d. Reproved

3. When we go to a party, we always <u>designate</u> a driver.

    a. Feign

    b. Exploit

    c. Dote

    d. Appoint

4. She went to Asia on $10 a day – her <u>frugal</u> travelling plans are amazing.

    a. Frothy

    b. Thrifty

    c. Fraught

    d. Focal

5. The warehouse went bankrupt so all of the furniture has to be <u>sold</u>.

    a. Dissected

    b. Liquidated

    c. Destroyed

    d. Bought

6. He sold the property when he didn't even own it. The whole thing was a <u>fraud</u>.

    a. Hoax

    b. Feign

    c. Defile

    d. Default

7. Just because she is supervisor, doesn't mean we have to <u>cower</u> in front of her.

    a. Foible

    b. Grovel

    c. Humiliate

    d. Indispose

8. That noise is <u>unbearable</u>! It is driving me crazy.

    a. Loud

    b. Intolerable

    c. Frivolous

    d. Fictitious

9. I see that sign everywhere. It is much more <u>frequent</u> than I thought.

    a. Prelude

    b. Prevalent

    c. Ratify

    d. Rational

10. Her attitude was very <u>casual</u>.

    a. Idle

    b. Nonchalant

    c. Portly

    d. Portend

11. The machine <u>powderizes</u> the rock.

    a. Quells

    b. Pulverizes

    c. Eradicates

    d. Segments

12. The water in the pond has been sitting for so long it is <u>dead</u>.

    a. Stagnant

    b. Sediment

    c. Stupor

    d. Residue

13. She didn't listen to a thing and <u>rejected</u> all the objections.

    a. Manipulated

    b. Mired

    c. Furtive

    d. Rebuffed

14. Many of his business deals were very <u>shady</u>.

    a. Dogged

    b. Unethical

    c. Impartial

    d. Furtive

15. I am always so bored at her lectures. They are tedious and <u>commonplace</u>.

    a. Hapless

    b. Glib

    c. Futile

    d. Humdrum

16. He loaned me the money last month and is going to repay tomorrow.

    a. Reimburse

    b. Reinstate

    c. Reconcile

    d. Rebuff

17. They will never give you your money back because they aren't a honourable company.

    a. Ravenous

    b. Rational

    c. Reformatory

    d. Reputable

18. After I took the medication I was so spaced out I wandered around in a daze.

    a. Quandary

    b. Solvent

    c. Stupor

    d. Reverie

19. After he damaged the house, he had to remedy the situation.

    a. Qualm

    b. Necessitate

    c. Rectify

    d. Narrate

20. She keeps gaining weight and grows more <u>over-weight</u> all the time.

    a. Piteous

    b. Portly

    c. Morbid

    d. Mystical

21. When Mr. Davis returned from southern Asia, he told us about the _____ that sometimes swept the area, bringing torrential rain.

    a. Monsoons

    b. Hurricanes

    c. Blizzards

    d. Floods

22. Is it true that _____ always grows on the north side of trees?

    a. Lichens

    b. Moss

    c. Ferns

    d. Ground cover

23. You can _____ some fires by covering them with dirt, while others require foam or water.

    a. Extinguish

    b. Distinguish

    c. Ignite

    d. Lessen

24. Through the use of powerful fans that circulate the heat over the food, _____ ovens work very efficiently.

    a. Microwave

    b. Broiler

    c. Convection

    d. Pressure

25. Because of the growing use of _____ as a fuel, corn production has greatly increased.

    a. Alcohol

    b. Ethanol

    c. Natural gas

    d. Oil

26. In heavily industrialized areas, the pollution of the air causes many to develop _____ diseases.

    a. Respiratory

    b. Cardiac

    c. Alimentary

    d. Circulatory

27. Because hydroelectric power is a _____ source of energy, its use is excellent for the environment.

    a. Significant

    b. Disposable

    c. Renewable

    d. Reusable

28. The process required the use of highly _____ liquids, so fire extinguishers were everywhere in the factory.

    a. Erratic

    b. Combustible

    c. Inflammable

    d. Neutral

29. She kept _____ him to do more and more.

    a. Push

    b. Force

    c. Threaten

    d. Goad

30. I was shocked by the _____ crime.

    a. Pleasantries

    b. Heinous

    c. Shrewd

    d. Provencal

31. The ballet dancer's performance was _____.

    a. Impeccable

    b. Formidable

    c. Genteel

    d. Disputation

32. The _____ now rules the country after a coup.

    a. Retribution

    b. Counsel

    c. Virago

    d. Junta

33. He has been sick for a year with this _____.

    a. Treatment

    b. Frontal

    c. Malady

    d. Assiduous

34. We couldn't sleep because of the _____ from the party next door.

    a. Nosy

    b. Racket

    c. Ravage

    d. Noisome

35. The _____ of quantum physics is some things are true and false at the same time.

    a. Inbred

    b. Paradox

    c. Attribute

    d. Fealty

**36. She complains all the time. I have never met any-
one so _____.**

    a. Querulous

    b. Complaint

    c. Compound

    d. Vestige

37. He fell into the _____ while skiing.

    a. Rumbling

    b. Ravine

    c. Delectable

    d. Distraught

**38. Everyone had to agree so the vote had to be
_____.**

    a. Ambiguous

    b. Unanimous

    c. Adulate

    d. Incredulous

39. We can edit out all of the unnecessary _____.

    a. Verbiage

    b. Outspoken

    c. Inveigh

    d. Precarious

40. They built an iron _____ for the grape vines to grow on.

    a. Farm

    b. Piggery

    c. Klink

    d. Vinery

READING COMPREHENSION.

Directions: The following questions are based on a number of reading passages. Each passage is followed by a series of questions. Read each passage carefully, and then answer the questions based on it. You may reread the passage as often as you wish. When you have finished answering the questions based on one passage, go right on to the next passage. Choose the best answer based on the information given and implied.

Questions 1-4 refer to the following passage.

Passage 1 - The Respiratory System

The respiratory system's function is to allow oxygen exchange through all parts of the body. The anatomy or structure of the exchange system, and the uses of the exchanged gases, varies depending on the organism. In humans and other mammals, for example, the anatomical features of the respiratory system include airways, lungs, and the respiratory muscles. Molecules of oxygen and carbon dioxide are passively exchanged, by diffusion, between the gaseous external environment and the blood. This exchange process occurs in the alveolar region of the lungs.

Other animals, such as insects, have respiratory systems with very simple anatomical features, and in amphibians even the skin plays a vital role in gas exchange. Plants also have respiratory systems but the direction of gas exchange can be opposite to that of animals.

The respiratory system can also be divided into physiological, or functional, zones. These include the conducting zone (the region for gas transport from the outside atmosphere to just above the alveoli), the transitional zone, and the respiratory zone (the alveolar region where gas exchange occurs). [15]

1. What can we infer from the first paragraph in this passage?

    a. Human and mammal respiratory systems are the same

    b. The lungs are an important part of the respiratory system

    c. The respiratory system varies in different mammals

    d. Oxygen and carbon dioxide are passive exchanged by the respiratory system

2. What is the process by which molecules of oxygen and carbon dioxide are passively exchanged?

    a. Transfusion

    b. Affusion

    c. Diffusion

    d. Respiratory confusion

3. What organ plays an important role in gas exchange in amphibians?

    a. The skin

    b. The lungs

    c. The gills

    d. The mouth

4. What are the three physiological zones of the respiratory system?

    a. Conducting, transitional, respiratory zones

    b. Redacting, transitional, circulatory zones

    c. Conducting, circulatory, inhibiting zones

    d. Transitional, inhibiting, conducting zones

Questions 5-8 refer to the following passage.

ABC Electric Warranty

ABC Electric Company warrants that its products are free from defects in material and workmanship. Subject to the conditions and limitations set forth below, ABC Electric will, at its option, either repair or replace any part of its products that prove defective due to improper workmanship or materials.

This limited warranty does not cover any damage to the product from improper installation, accident, abuse, misuse, natural disaster, insufficient or excessive electrical supply, abnormal mechanical or environmental conditions, or any unauthorized disassembly, repair, or modification.

This limited warranty also does not apply to any product on which the original identification information has been altered, or removed, has not been handled or packaged correctly, or has been sold as second-hand.

This limited warranty covers only repair, replacement, refund or credit for defective ABC Electric products, as provided above.

5. I tried to repair my ABC Electric blender, but could not, so can I get it repaired under this warranty?

   a. Yes, the warranty still covers the blender

   b. No, the warranty does not cover the blender

   c. Uncertain. ABC Electric may or may not cover repairs under this warranty

6. My ABC Electric fan is not working. Will ABC Electric provide a new one or repair this one?

   a. ABC Electric will repair my fan

   b. ABC Electric will replace my fan

   c. ABC Electric could either replace or repair my fan can request either a replacement or a repair.

7. My stove was damaged in a flood. Does this warranty cover my stove?

   a. Yes, it is covered.

   b. No, it is not covered.

   c. It may or may not be covered.

   d. ABC Electric will decide if it is covered

8. Which of the following is an example of improper workmanship?

   a. Missing parts

   b. Defective parts

   c. Scratches on the front

   d. None of the above

Questions 9 – 12 refer to the following passage.

Passage 3 – Mythology

The main characters in myths are usually gods or super-natural heroes. As sacred stories, rulers and priests have traditionally endorsed their myths and as a result, myths have a close link with religion and politics. In the society where a myth originates, the natives believe the myth is a true account of the remote past. In fact, many societies have two categories of traditional narrative—(1) "true stories", or myths, and (2) "false stories", or fables.

Myths generally take place during a primordial age, when the world was still young, prior to achieving its current form. These stories explain how the world gained its current form and why the culture developed its customs, institutions, and taboos. Closely related to myth are legend and folktale. Myths, legends, and folktales are different types of traditional stories. Unlike myths, folktales can take place at any time and any place, and the natives do not usually consider them true or sacred. Legends, on the other hand, are similar to myths in that many people have traditionally considered them true. Legends take place in a more recent time, when the world was much as it is today. In addition, legends generally feature humans as their main characters, whereas myths have superhuman characters. [16]

9. We can infer from this passage that

a. Folktales took place in a time far past, before civilization covered the earth

b. Humankind uses myth to explain how the world was created

c. Myths revolve around gods or supernatural beings; the local community usually accepts these stories as not true

d. The only difference between a myth and a legend is the time setting of the story

10. The main purpose of this passage is

a. To distinguish between many types of traditional stories, and explain the back-ground of some traditional story categories

b. To determine whether myths and legends might be true accounts of history

c. To show the importance of folktales how these traditional stories made life more bearable in harder times

d. None of the Above

11. How are folktales different from myths?

a. Folktales and myth are the same

b. Folktales are not true and generally not sacred and take place anytime

c. Myths are not true and generally not sacred and take place anytime

d. Folktales explained the formation of the world and myths do not

12. How are legends and myth similar?

a. Many people believe legends and myths are true, myths take place in modern day, and legends are about ordinary people

b. Many people believe legends and myths are true, legends take place in modern day, and legends are about ordinary people

c. Many people believe legends and myths are true, legends take place in modern day, and myths are about ordinary people

d. Many people believe legends and myths are not true, legends take place in mod-ern day, and legends are about ordinary people

Questions 13-18 refer to the following passage.

Passage 4 – Myths, Legend and Folklore

Cultural historians draw a distinction between myth, legend and folktale simply as a way to group traditional stories. However, in many cultures, drawing a sharp line between myths and legends is not that simple. Instead of dividing their traditional stories into myths, legends, and folktales, some cultures divide them into two categories. The first category roughly corresponds to folktales, and the second is one that combines myths and legends. Similarly, we can not always separate myths from folktales. One society might consider a story true, making it a myth. Another society might understand the story is fictional, which makes it a folktale. In fact, when a myth loses its status as part of a religious system, it often takes on traits more typical of folktales, with its formerly divine characters now appearing as human heroes, giants, or fairies. Myth, legend, and folktale are only a few of the categories of traditional stories. Other categories include anecdotes and some kinds of jokes. Traditional stories, in turn, are only one category within the much larger category of folklore, which also includes items such as gestures, costumes, and music. [16]

13. The main idea of this passage is that

a. Myths, fables, and folktales are not the same thing, and each describes a specific type of story

b. Traditional stories can be categorized in different ways by different people

c. Cultures use myths for religious purposes, and when this is no longer true, the people forget and discard these myths

d. Myths can never become folk tales, because one is true, and the other is false

14. The terms myth and legend are

a. Categories that are synonymous with true and false

b. Categories that group traditional stories according to certain characteristics

c. Interchangeable, because both terms mean a story that is passed down from generation to generation

d. Meant to distinguish between a story that involves a hero and a cultural message and a story meant only to entertain

15. Traditional story categories not only include myths and legends, but

a. Can also include gestures, since some cultures passed these down before the written and spoken word

b. In addition, folklore refers to stories involving fables and fairy tales

c. These story categories can also include folk music and traditional dress

d. Traditional stories themselves are a part of the larger category of folklore, which may also include costumes, gestures, and music

16. This passage shows that

a. There is a distinct difference between a myth and a legend, although both are folktales

b. Myths are folktales, but folktales are not myths

c. Myths, legends, and folktales play an important part in tradition and the past, and are a rich and colorful part of history

d. Most cultures consider myths as true

Questions 17-19 refer to the following passage.

Passage 5 – Insects

Humans regard certain insects as pests and attempt to control them with insecticides and many other techniques. Some insects damage crops by feeding on sap, leaves or fruits, a few bite humans and livestock, alive and dead, to feed on blood and some are capable of transmitting diseases to humans, pets and live-stock. Many other insects are considered ecologically beneficial and a few provide direct economic benefit. Silkworms and bees, for example, have been domesticated for the production of silk and honey, respectively. [17]

17. How do humans control insects?

a. By training them

b. Using insecticides and other techniques

c. In many different ways

d. Humans do not control insects

18. Why do humans control insects?

    a. Because they do not like them

    b. Because they damage crops

    c. Because they damage buildings

    d. Because they damage the soil

19. How do insects damage crops?

    a. By feeding on crops

    b. By transmitting disease

    c. By laying eggs on crops

    d. None of the above

Questions 20-24 refer to the following passage.

Passage 6 – Trees I

Trees are an important part of the natural landscape because they prevent erosion and protect ecosystems in and under their branches. Trees also play an important role in producing oxygen and reducing carbon dioxide in the atmosphere, as well as moderating ground temperatures. Trees are important elements in landscaping and agriculture, both for their visual appeal and for their crops, such as apples, and other fruit. Wood from trees is a building material, and a primary energy source in many developing countries. Trees also play a role in many of the world's mythologies. [18]

20. What are two reasons trees are important in the natural landscape?

    a. They prevent erosion and produce oxygen

    b. They produce fruit and are important elements in landscaping

    c. Trees are not important in the natural landscape

    d. Trees produce carbon dioxide and prevent erosion

21. What kind of ecosystems do trees protect?

    a. Trees do not protect ecosystems

    b. Weather sheltered ecosystems

    c. Ecosystems around the base and under the branches

    d. All of the above

22. Which of the following is true?

    a. Trees provide a primary food source in the developing world

    b. Trees provide a primary building material in the developing world

    c. Trees provide a primary energy source in the developing world

    d. Trees provide a primary oxygen source in the developing world

23. Why are trees important for agriculture?

    a. Because of their crops

    b. Because they shelter ecosystems

    c. Because they are a source of energy

    d. Because of their visual appeal

24. What do trees do to the atmosphere?

a. Trees produce carbon dioxide and reduce oxygen

b. Trees product oxygen and carbon dioxide

c. Trees reduce oxygen and carbon dioxide

d. Trees produce oxygen and reduce carbon dioxide

Questions 25-28 refer to the following passage.

Passage 7 – Trees II

With an estimated 100,000 species, trees represent 25 percent of all living plant species. The majority of tree species grow in tropical regions of the world and many of these areas have not been surveyed by botanists, making species diversity poorly understood. The earliest trees were tree ferns and horsetails, which grew in forests in the Carboniferous period. Tree ferns still survive, but the only surviving horsetails are no longer in tree form. Later, in the Triassic period, conifers and ginkgos, appeared, followed by flowering plants after that in the Cretaceous period. [18]

25. Do botanists understand the number of tree species?

a. Yes botanists know exactly how many tree species there are

b. No, the species diversity is not well understood

c. Yes, botanists are sure

d. No, botanists have no idea

26. Where do most trees species grow?

    a. Most tree species grow in tropical regions.

    b. There is no one area where most tree species grow.

    c. Tree species grow in 25% of the world.

    d. There are 100,000 tree species.

27. What tree(s) survived from the Carboniferous period?

    a. 25% of all trees.

    b. Horsetails.

    c. Conifers.

    d. Tree Ferns.

28. Choose the correct list below, ranked from oldest to youngest trees.

    a. Flowering plants, conifers and ginkgos, tree ferns and horsetails.

    b. Tree ferns and horsetails, conifers and ginkgos, flowering plants.

    c. Tree ferns and horsetails, flowering plants, conifers and ginkgos.

    d. Conifers and ginkgos, tree ferns and horsetails, flowering plants.

Questions 29 - 30 refer to the following passage.

Lowest Price Guarantee

Get it for less. Guaranteed!

ABC Electric will beat any advertised price by 10% of the difference.

1) If you find a lower advertised price, we will beat it by 10% of the difference.

2) If you find a lower advertised price within 30 days* of your purchase we will beat it by 10% of the difference.

3) If our own price is reduced within 30 days* of your purchase, bring in your receipt and we will refund the difference.

*14 days for computers, monitors, printers, laptops, tablets, cellular & wireless devices, home security products, projectors, camcorders, digital cameras, radar detectors, portable DVD players, DJ and pro-audio equipment, and air conditioners.

29. I bought a radar detector 15 days ago and saw an ad for the same model only cheaper. Can I get 10% of the difference refunded?

a. Yes. Since it is less than 30 days, you can get 10% of the difference refunded.

b. No. Since it is more than 14 days, you cannot get 10% of the difference re-funded.

c. It depends on the cashier.

d. Yes. You can get the difference refunded.

30. I bought a flat-screen TV for $500 10 days ago and found an advertisement for the same TV, at another store, on sale for $400. How much will ABC refund under this guarantee?

a. $100

b. $110

c. $10

d. $400

Part III – English Grammar and Usage.

1. Choose the sentence with the correct usage.

a. Vegetables are a healthy food; eating them can make you more healthful.

b. Vegetables are a healthful food; eating them can make you more healthful.

c. Vegetables are a healthy food; eating them can make you more healthy.

d. Vegetables are a healthful food; eating them can make you more healthy.

2. Choose the sentence with the correct usage.

a. After you lay the books on the counter, you may lay down for a nap.

b. After you lie the books on the counter, you may lay down for a nap.

c. After you lay the books on the counter, you may lie down for a nap.

d. After you lay the books on the counter, you may lay down for a nap.

3. Choose the sentence with the correct usage.

a. Once the chickens had layed their eggs, they lay on their nests to hatch them.

b. Once the chickens had lay their eggs, they lay on their nests to hatch them.

c. Once the chickens had laid their eggs, they lay on their nests to hatch them.

d. Once the chickens had laid their eggs, they laid on their nests to hatch them.

4. Choose the sentence with the correct usage.

a. Mrs. Foster taught me many things, but I learned the most from Mr. Wallace.

b. Mrs. Foster learned me many things, but I was taught the most by Mr. Wallace.

c. Mrs. Foster learned me many things, but I learned the most from Mr. Wallace.

d. Mrs. Foster taught me many things, but I was learned the most from Mr. Wallace.

5. Choose the sentence with the correct usage.

a. He did not have to loose the race; if only his shoes weren't so lose!

b. He did not have to lose the race; if only his shoes weren't so loose!

c. He did not have to lose the race; if only his shoes weren't so lose!

d. He did not have to loose the race; if only his shoes weren't so loose!

6. Choose the sentence with the correct usage.

a. The attorney did not want to prosecute the defendant; his goal was to prosecute the guilty party.

b. The attorney did not want to persecute the defendant; his goal was to persecute the guilty party.

c. The attorney did not want to prosecute the defendant; his goal was to persecute the guilty party.

d. The attorney did not want to persecute the defendant; his goal was to prosecute the guilty party.

7. Choose the sentence with the correct usage.

a. The speeches must precede the election; the election cannot proceed without hearing from the candidates.

b. The speeches must precede the election; the election cannot precede without hearing from the candidates.

c. The speeches must proceed the election; the election cannot precede without hearing from the candidates.

d. The speeches must proceed the election; the election cannot proceed without hearing from the candidates.

8. Choose the sentence with the correct usage.

a. Before a lawyer can rise an objection, he must first rise to his feet.

b. Before a lawyer can raise an objection, he must first raise to his feet.

c. Before a lawyer can raise an objection, he must first rise to his feet.

d. Before a lawyer can rise an objection, he must first raise to his feet.

9. Choose the sentence with the correct usage.

a. You shouldn't sit in that chair wearing black pants; I set the white cat there just a moment ago.

b. You shouldn't set in that chair wearing black pants; I sit the white cat there just a moment ago.

c. You shouldn't set in that chair wearing black pants; I set the white cat there just a moment ago.

d. You shouldn't sit in that chair wearing black pants; I sit the white cat there just a moment ago.

For Each Of The Sentences Below Choose The Correct Word To Replace The Underlined Word Or Phrase.

10. The teacher told us yesterday the sun <u>was</u> bigger than Earth.

    a. is the

    b. is

    c. was the

    d. none of the above

11. Please <u>die</u> this cloth.

    a. died

    b. dye

    c. dyed

    d. none of the above

Fill in the Blanks.

12. Our office is a four _____ building.

    a. storey

    b. storys

    c. story

    d. none of the above

13. The government didn't have the _____ idea what to do.

    a. finest

    b. faintest

    c. fairest

    d. none of the above.

14. His father is _____.

    a. a poet and novelist

    b. poet and novelist

    c. a poet and a novelist

    d. none of the above

15. In Edgar Allen Poe's _____ Edgar Allen Poe describes a man with a guilty conscience.

    a. short story, "The Tell-Tale Heart,"

    b. short story The Tell-Tale Heart,

    c. short story, The Tell-Tale Heart

    d. short story. "the Tell-Tale Heart,"

16. Billboards are considered an important part of advertising for big business, _____ by their critics.

    a. but, an eyesore;

    b. but, " an eyesore,"

    c. but an eyesore

    d. but-an eyesore-

17. I can never remember how to use those two common words, "sell," meaning to trade a product for money, or _____ meaning an event where products are traded for less money than usual.

    a. sale-

    b. "sale,"

    c. "sale

    d. "to sale,"

18. The class just finished reading _____ a short story by Carl Stephenson about a plantation owner's battle with army ants.

    a. -"Leinengen versus the Ants",

    b. Leinengen versus the Ants,

    c. "Leinengen versus the Ants,"

    d. Leinengen versus the Ants

19. After the car was fixed, it _____ again.

    a. ran good

    b. ran well

    c. would have run well

    d. ran more well

20. Choose the sentence with the correct grammar.

    a. There was scarcely no food in the pantry, because nobody ate at home.

    b. There was scarcely any food in the pantry, because nobody ate at home.

    c. There was scarcely any food in the pantry, because not nobody ate at home.

    d. There was scarcely no food in the pantry, because not nobody ate at home.

21. Choose the sentence with the correct grammar.

a. Although you may not see nobody in the dark, it does not mean that nobody is there.

b. Although you may not see anyone in the dark, it does not mean that not nobody is there.

c. Although you may not see anyone in the dark, it does not mean that no one is there.

d. Although you may not see nobody in the dark, it does not mean that not nobody is there.

22. Choose the sentence with the correct grammar.

a. Michael has lived in that house for forty years, while I has owned this one for only six weeks.

b. Michael have lived in that house for forty years, while I have owned this one for only six weeks.

c. Michael have lived in that house for forty years, while I has owned this one for only six weeks.

d. Michael has lived in that house for forty years, while I have owned this one for only six weeks.

23. Choose the sentence with the correct grammar.

a. The older children have already eat their dinner, but the baby has not yet eaten anything.

b. The older children have already eaten their dinner, but the baby has not yet ate anything.

c. The older children have already eaten their dinner, but the baby has not yet eaten anything.

d. The older children have already eat their dinner, but the baby has not yet ate anything.

24. Choose the sentence with the correct grammar.

a. If they had gone to the party, he would have gone, too.

b. If they had went to the party, he would have gone, too.

c. If they had gone to the party, he would have went, too.

d. If they had went to the party, he would have went, too.

25. Choose the sentence with the correct grammar.

a. He should have went to the appointment; instead, he went to the beach.

b. He should have gone to the appointment; instead, he went to the beach.

c. He should have went to the appointment; instead, he gone to the beach.

d. He should have gone to the appointment; instead, he gone to the beach.

26. Choose the sentence with the correct grammar.

a. Lee pronounced it's name incorrectly; it's an impatiens, not an impatience.

b. Lee pronounced its name incorrectly; its an impatiens, not an impatience.

c. Lee pronounced it's name incorrectly; its an impatiens, not an impatience.

d. Lee pronounced its name incorrectly; it's an impatiens, not an impatience.

27. Choose the sentence with the correct grammar.

a. Its important for you to know its official name; its called the Confederate Museum.

b. It's important for you to know it's official name; it's called the Confederate Museum.

c. It's important for you to know its official name; it's called the Confederate Museum.

d. Its important for you to know it's official name; it's called the Confederate Museum.

28. As the tallest monument in the United States, the St. Louis Arch _____.

a. has rose to an impressive 630 feet.

b. is risen to an impressive 630 feet.

c. rises to an impressive 630 feet.

d. was rose to an impressive 630 feet.

29. The tired, old woman should _____ on the sofa.

a. lie

b. lays

c. laid

d. lain

30. Did the students understand that Thanksgiving always _____ on the fourth Thursday in November?

a. fallen

b. falling

c. has fell

d. falls

31. Collecting stamps, _____ and listening to shortwave radio were Rick's main hobbies.

    a. building models,

    b. to build models,

    c. having built models,

    d. build models,

32. This morning, _____ and before the sun came up, my mother makes herself a cup of cocoa.

    a. after the kids had left for school

    b. after the kids leave for school

    c. after the kids have left for school

    d. after the kids will leave for school

33. Elaine promised to bring the camera _____ at the mall yesterday.

    a. by me

    b. with me

    c. at me

    d. to me

34. Last night, he _____ the sleeping bag down beside my mattress.

    a. lay

    b. laid

    c. lain

    d. has laid

35. I would have bought the shirt for you if _____.

    a. I had known you liked it

    b. I have known you liked it

    c. I would know you liked it

    d. I know you liked it

36. Many believers still hope _____ proof of the existence of ghosts.

    a. two find

    b. to find

    c. to found

    d. to have been found

37. Our office is a four _____ building.

    a. storey

    b. storys

    c. story

    d. none of the above

38. The government didn't have the _____ idea what to do.

    a. finest

    b. faintest

    c. fairest

    d. none of the above.

39. His father is _____.

    a. a poet and novelist

    b. poet and novelist

    c. a poet and a novelist

    d. none of the above

40. Please excuse _____ late.

    a. me for late

    b. being late

    c. being

    d. The sentence is correct

PART IV - CLOZE

PASSAGE 1 - THE JUNGLE BOOK – TOOMAI THE ELEPHANT.

Kala Nag, which means Black Snake, ___1___ served the Indian Government in every way that ___2___ elephant could serve it for forty-seven years, and as he was twenty years old ___3___ he was caught, that makes him nearly seventy—a ripe age for an elephant. He remembered ___4___, with a big leather pad ___5___ his forehead, at a gun stuck in deep mud, and that was before the Afghan War of 1842, and he had not then come to his full strength.

His mother Radha Pyari,—Radha the darling,—who had been caught at the same time with Kala Nag, ___6___ him, that elephants ___7___ were afraid always got hurt. Kala Nag knew this advice ___8___ good, for the first time that he saw a shell burst he backed, screaming, into a stand of piled rifles, and the bayonets pricked him in all his softest places. So, before he was twenty-five, he gave up being afraid, and so he was the best-loved and the best-looked-after elephant in the service of the Government of India. [19]

1.

    a. had

    b. has

2.

    a. a

    b. an

3.

    a. at

    b. when

4.

    a. pushing

    b. pushes

5.

    a. on

    b. at

6.

    a. told

    b. tells

7.

    a. that

    b. who

8.

    a. knew

    b. had known

PASSAGE 2 - WHO STOLE THE TARTS?

The King and Queen of Hearts were seated on their throne when they ___9___, with a great crowd assembled around them—all sorts of little birds and beasts, ___10___ the whole pack of cards: the Knave was standing before them, in chains, ___11___ a soldier on each side to guard him; and near the King ___12___ the White Rabbit, with a trumpet in one hand, and a scroll of parchment in the other. In the very middle of the court was a table, with a large dish of tarts ___13___ it: they looked so good, that it made Alice quite hungry to look at them—'I wish they'd get the trial done,' she___14___, 'and hand round the refreshments!' But ___15___ seemed to be no chance of this, so she began looking at everything about her, to pass the time.

Alice ___**16**___ in a court of justice before, but she had read about them in books, and she was quite pleased to find that she knew the name of nearly everything there. '___**17**___ the judge,' she said to herself, 'because of his big wig.'

The judge, ___**18**___, was the King; and as he wore his crown over the wig, he did not look comfortable, and it was certainly not becoming.

'And that's the jury-box,' thought Alice, 'and those twelve creatures,' (she was obliged to say 'creatures,' you see, because some of them were animals, and some were birds,) 'I ___**19**___ they are the jurors.' She ___**20**___ this last word two or three times to herself, being rather proud of it: for she thought, very few little girls of her age knew the meaning of it at all.[14]

9.

    a. arrived

    b. arrive

10.

    a. because of

    b. as well as

11.

    a. with

    b. and

12.

    a. was

    b. is

13.

    a. over

    b. on

14.

    a. thought

    b. thinks

15.

    a. there

    b. their

16.

> a. was never
> b. had never been

17.

> a. That's
> b. thats'

18.

> a. by the way
> b. in addition to

19.

> a. think
> b. suppose

20.

> a. said
> b. says

ANSWER KEY

PART 1 - VOCABULARY

1. D
Conclusive: Providing an end to something; decisive.

2. C
Dupe: To swindle, deceive, or trick.

3. D
Designate: appointed; chosen.

4. B
Frugal: cheap, economical, thrifty.

5. B
Liquidate: to convert assets into cash.

6. A
Hoax: To deceive (someone) by making them believe something which has been maliciously or mischievously fabricated.

7. B
Grovel: To abase oneself before another person.

8. B
Intolerable: not capable of being borne or endured; not proper or right to be allowed; insufferable; insupportable; unbearable.

9. B
Prevalent: Widespread.

10. B
Nonchalant: Casually calm and relaxed.

11. B
Pulverizes: to completely destroy, especially by crushing to fragments or a powder.

12. A
Stagnant: lacking freshness, motion, flow, progress, or change; stale; motionless; still.

13. D
Rebuff: a sudden resistance or refusal.

14. B
Unethical: morally bad; not ethical.

15. D
Humdrum: lacking variety or excitement; dull; boring.

16. A
Reimburse: to compensate with pay or money; especially, to repay money spent on one's behalf.

17. D
Reputable: having a good reputation; honourable.

18. C
Stupor: a state in which one has difficulty in thinking or using one's senses.

19. C
Rectify: to correct or amend something.

20. B
Portly: euphemism for fat

21. A
Monsoons: Tropical rainy season when the rain lasts for several months

22. B
Moss: Any of various small green plants growing on the ground or on the surfaces of trees, stones etc.;

23. A
Extinguish: to put out, as in fire; to end burning; to quench.

24. C
Convection: The transmission of heat in a fluid or gas by the circulation of currents.

25. B
Ethanol: A simple alcohol derived from ethane.

26. A
Respiratory: relating to respiration; breathing.

27. D
Reusable: Able to be used multiple times.

28. B
Combustible: A material that is capable of burning.

29. A
Goad: to encourage, stimulate or incite and provoke.

30. B
Heinous: adj. shocking, terrible or wicked.

31. A
Impeccable: adj. perfect, no faults or errors.

32. D
Junta: n. ruling council of a military government.

33. C
Malady: n. a lingering disease or ailment of the human body.

34. D
Racket: A loud noise.

35. B
Paradox: a self contradictory statement that can only be true if false and vice versa.

36. A
Querulous: Often complaining; suggesting a complaint in expression; fretful, whining.

37. B
Ravine: A deep narrow valley or gorge in the earth's surface worn by running water.

38. B
Unanimous: complete agreement or harmony

39. A
Verbiage: speech with too many words

40. D
A structure, usually enclosed with glass, for rearing and protecting vines. [4]

Part II - READing Comprehension

1. B
We can infer **an important part of the respiratory system are the lungs.**

2. C
The process by which molecules of oxygen and carbon dioxide are passively exchanged is **diffusion**.

3. A
The organ plays an important role in gas exchange in amphibians is **the skin.**

4. A
The three physiological zones of the respiratory system are **conducting, transitional, respiratory zones.**

5. B
A preheated oven is an oven heated to the correct temperature, in this case, 350 degrees F (175 degrees C).

6. C
The mixture will need to be stirred 6 times. From the instructions,

Bring to a boil, and cook for 3 minutes, stirring every 30 seconds.

7. A
"Pat" in this sentence means to

Spread the filling over the base, and pat the remaining crumb mixture on top.

8. B
The total brown sugar is 1 1/3 cups.

1 1/2 cups rolled oats
1 1/2 cups sifted pastry flour
1/4 teaspoon salt
3/4 teaspoon baking soda
1 cup packed brown sugar
3/4 cup butter, softened

3/4 pound pitted dates, diced
1 cup water
1/3 cup packed brown sugar
1 teaspoon lemon juice

9. B
The first paragraph tells us that myths are a true account of the remote past.

The second paragraph tells us that, "myths generally take place during a primordial age, when the world was still young, prior to achieving its current form."

Putting these two together, we can infer that **mankind used myth to explain how the world was created.**

10. A
This passage is about different types of stories. First the passage explains myths, and then compares other types of stories to myths.

11. B
From the passage, "Unlike myths, folktales can take place

at any time and any place, and the natives do not usually consider them true or sacred."

12. B
This question gives options with choices for the 3 different characteristics of myth and legend. The options are,

True or not true
Takes place in modern day
About ordinary people

For this type of question, where two things are compared for different characteristics, you can easily eliminate wrong answers using only one of the choices. Take myths: myths are believed to be true, do not take place in modern day, and are not about ordinary people.

Make a list as in,

True or not true - True
Takes place in modern day - No
About ordinary people - No

Now checking the options quickly. Option A is wrong (myths don't take place in modern day). Option B looks good. Put a check beside it.   Option C is wrong (myths are about ordinary people), and Option D is wrong (myths are not true), so the answer must be Option B.

13. A
Myths, fables, and folktales are not the same thing, and each describes a specific type of story that is traditional.

14. B
Tools that allow traditional stories to be grouped according to certain categories.

15. D
Traditional stories themselves are a category of folklore, which may also include costumes and gestures among others.

16. C
Myths, Legends, and folktales play an important part in tradition and the past, and they are a rich and colorful part of history.

17. B
Myths are based on stories about gods and people with super human qualities, instead of super exploits by mere mortals and humans.

18. A
It may be hard to distinguish between myths, legends, and folktales, and what may be a myth to one culture may be a legend or folktale to another culture.

19. B

20. B
The inference is humans control pests because they damage crops.

21. A
Feeding on crops is the best choice, even though a. and c. are also correct.

22. A
This choice is a re-wording of text from the passage.

23. B
The answer is taken directly from the passage.

24. C
Although trees are used as a building material, this is not their primary use. Trees are a primary energy source.

25. A
The answer is taken directly from the passage.

26. D
This question is designed to confuse. Read the passage carefully to see which is reduced and which is produced.

27. B
The time limit for radar detectors is 14 days. Since you made the purchase 15 days ago, you do not qualify for the guarantee.

28. B
Since you made the purchase 10 days ago, you are covered by the guarantee. Since it is an advertised price at a different store, ABC Electric will 'beat' the price by 10% of the difference, which is,

500 – 400 = 100 – difference in price
100 X 10% = $10 – 10% of the difference

The advertised lower price is $400. ABC will beat this price by 10% so they will refund $100 + 10 = $110

29. B
Since the purchase was 12 days ago, and the same store advertised the same model, you will qualify for the full difference in price refunded.

The difference will be, 250 – 199 = $51

30. B
According to the guarantee, #1,

1) If you find a lower advertised price, we will beat it by 10% of the difference.

$650 – 599 = $51
51 X 10% = $5.10

The answer will be the lower advertised price ($599) minus 10% of the difference ($5.10), which is $593.90.

SECTION III – ENGLISH GRAMMAR AND USAGE

1. D
"Healthy" describes people or animals that are in good health. "Healthful" is generally used in formal speech or writing, and refers to things that are good for health. "In" is a preposition that refers to being inside of something. "Into" refers to the action of entering. It should be noted, however, that in many cases either word can be used.

2. C
"Lie" does not require a direct object, while "lay" does. In this sentence, "lay" is followed by the direct object, "the books."

3. C
This is the correct choice.

4. B
"Learn" means to receive and integrate knowledge or an experience. "Teach" means to impart knowledge to another.

5. B
"Lose" is a verb meaning to misplace something or to fail at a competition. "Loose" is an adjective meaning untied or able to move freely.

6. D
"Prosecute" means to begin legal proceedings against an individual or group. "Persecute" is to harass.

7. A
"Precede" means to go first or in front of others. "Proceed" means to go forward, or to begin something.

8. C
"Rise," like other intransitive verbs, is used without an object; the subject does the action on its own. For example, "The sun rises." "Raise" is a transitive verb, and is used for actions that cannot be done by a subject alone

but needs an object. For example, "The student raised her hand."

9. A

"Sit," like other intransitive verbs, is used without an object; the subject does the action on its own. For example, "When told to, the dog sits." "Set" is a transitive verb, and is used for actions that cannot be done by a subject alone but needs an object to complete the action. For example, "The student set her books on the table."

10. B

Even though the conversation occurred in the past, "is" is correct since it refers to an unchanging state of being.

11. B

"Dye" mean to change the color of something by means of a stain or chemical process; "die" means to pass away.

12. C

"Story," when used as an adjective modifying a building, is singular.

13. B

"Faintest" means least. "Finest" means the best. "Fairest" is the most fair.

14. A

There is no need to repeat the article, "a," a second time.

15. A

Titles of short stories are enclosed in quotation marks.

16. C

No additional punctuation is required here.

17. B

Here the word "sale" is used as a "word" and not as a word in the sentence, so quotation marks are used.

18. C

Titles of short stories are enclosed in quotation marks, and commas always go inside quotation marks.

19. B
"Ran well" is correct. "Ran good" is never correct.

20. B
In double negative sentences, one of the negatives is replaced with "any."

21. C
In double negative sentences, one of the negatives is replaced with "any."

22. D
The present perfect tense cannot be used with specific time expressions such as yesterday, one year ago, last week, when I was a child, at that moment, that day, one day, etc. The present perfect tense is used with unspecific expressions such as ever, never, once, many times, several times, before, so far, already, yet, etc.

23. C
The present perfect tense cannot be used with specific time expressions such as yesterday, one year ago, last week, when I was a child, at that moment, that day, one day, etc. The present perfect tense is used with unspecific expressions such as ever, never, once, many times, several times, before, so far, already, yet, etc.

24. A
"Went" is used in the simple past tense. "Gone" is used in the past perfect tense.

25. B
"Went" is used in the simple past tense. "Gone" is used in the past perfect tense.

26. D
"It's" is a contraction for it is or it has. "Its" is a possessive pronoun.

27. C
"It's" is a contraction for it is or it has. "Its" is a possessive pronoun.

28. C

The simple present tense, "rises," is correct.

29. A

"Lie" does not require a direct object, while "lay" does. The old woman might lie on the couch, which has no direct object, or she might lay the book down, which has the direct object, "the book."

30. D

The simple present tense, "falls," is correct because it is repeated action.

31. A

The present progressive, "building models," is correct in this sentence; it is required to match the other present progressive verbs.

32. A

Past Perfect tense describes a completed action in the past, before another action in the past.

33. D

The preposition "to" is the correct preposition to use with "bring."

34. B

"Laid" is the past tense.

35. A

This is a past unreal conditional sentence. It requires an 'if' clause and a result clause, and either clause can appear first. The 'if' clause uses the past perfect, while the result clause uses the past participle.

36. B

"Hope" is followed by the infinitive; in this case, "to find."

37. C

"Story," when used as an adjective modifying a building, is singular.

38. B

"Faintest" means least. "Finest" means the best. "Fairest" is the most fair.

39. A

There is no need to repeat the article, "a," a second time.

40. C

"Please excuse my being late" has the same meaning as "Please excuse me for being late," and is correct.

Section IV - Cloze

1. A

The sentence is past perfect, since "served" is past tense, so "had served" is correct.

2. A

"Elephant" starts with a vowel, so "a" is correct.

3. B

The sentence refers to the time he was caught so "when" is correct.

4. A

The present continuous, "pushing" is correct.

5. A

The preposition "on" is correct.

6. A

The sentence is in the past tense, so "told" is correct.

7. B

The phrase refers to an individual, so "who" is correct.

8. A

The simple past tense "knew" is correct in this sentence.

9. A

Past tense is correct in this sentenced to agree with "seated."

10. B
The sentence uses "as well as" meaning in addition to, as "the whole pack of cards" is not related to the other items.

11. A
"With" means, Accompanied by (another person or thing).

12. A
"Was" is correct as the sentence is in the past tense.

13. B
"On" in this sentence means, in contact with and supported by a surface.

14. A
"Thought" is correct because the sentence is in the past tense.

15. A
There vs. their. There indicates existence as in, "there are." Their is to indicate possession, as in, "their book."

16. B
This sentence uses the past perfect. The past perfect form is used to describe an event that occurred in the past and prior to another event.

17. A
The contraction, "that's" or "that is" is correct in this sentence.

18. A
"By the way," is used in this sentence to talk about something that is connected to a previous topic.

19. B
"To suppose," is to guess.

20. A
The past tense "said" is correct.

How to Prepare for a Test

MOST STUDENTS HIDE THEIR HEADS AND PROCRASTI-NATE WHEN FACED WITH PREPARING FOR AN EXAM, HOPING THAT SOMEHOW THEY WILL BE SPARED THE AGONY, ESPECIALLY IF IT IS A BIG ONE THAT THEIR FUTURES RELY ON. Avoiding a test is what many students do best and unfortunately, they suffer the consequences because of their lack of preparation.

Test preparation requires strategy and dedication. It is the perfect training ground for a professional life. Besides having several reliable strategies, successful students also has a clear goal and know how to accomplish it. These tried and true concepts have worked well and will make your test preparation easier.

The Study Approach

Take responsibility for your own test preparation.

It is a common - but big - mistake to link your studying to someone else's. Study partners are great, but only if they are reliable. It is your job to be prepared for the test, even if a study partner fails you. Do not allow others to distract you from your goals.

Prioritize the time available to study

When do you learn best, early in the day or at night? Does your mind absorb and retain information most efficiently in small blocks of time, or do you require long stretches to get the most done? It is important to figure out the best blocks of time available to you when you can be the most productive. Try to consolidate activities to allow for longer periods of study time.

Find a quiet place where you will not be disturbed

Do not try to squeeze in quality study time in any old location. Find some place peaceful and with a minimum of distractions, such as the library, a park or even the laundry room. Good lighting is essential and you need to have comfortable seating and a desk surface large enough to hold your materials. It is probably not a great idea to study in your bedroom. You might be distracted by clothes on the floor, a book you have been planning to read, the telephone or something else. Besides, in the middle of studying, that bed will start to look very comfortable. Whatever you do, avoid using the bed as a place to study since you might fall asleep to avoiding studying!

The exception is flashcards. By far the most productive study time is sitting down and studying and studying only. However, with flashcards you can carry them with you and make use of odd moments, like standing in line or waiting for the bus. This isn't as productive, but it really helps and is definitely worth doing.

Determine what you need to study

Gather together your books, your notes, your laptop and any other materials needed to focus on your study for this exam. Ensure you have everything you need so you don't waste time. Remember paper, pencils and erasers, sticky notes, bottled water and a snack. Keep your phone with you if you need it to find essential information, but keep it turned off so others can't distract you.

Have a positive attitude

It is essential that you approach your studies for the test with an attitude that says you will pass it. And pass it with flying colors! This is one of the most important keys to successful studying. Believing that you are capable helps you to become capable.

The Strategy of Studying

Review class notes

Stay on top of class notes and assignments by reviewing them frequently and regularly. Re-writing notes can be a terrific study trick, as it helps lock in information. Pay special attention to any comments that have been made by the teacher. If a study guide has been made available as part of the class materials, use it! It will be a valuable tool to use for studying.

Estimate how much time you will need

If you are concerned about the amount of time you have available it is a good idea to set up a schedule so that you do not get bogged down on one section and end without enough time left to study other things. Remember to schedule break time, and use that time for a little exercise or other stress reducing techniques.

Test yourself to determine your weaknesses

Look online for additional assessment and evaluation tools available for a particular subject. Visit our website http://www.test-preparation.ca for test tips and more practice questions. Once you have determined areas of concern, you will be able to focus on studying the information they contain and just brush up on the other areas of the exam.

Mental Prep – How to Psych Yourself Up for a Test

Since tests are often a big factor in your final grade or acceptance into a program, it is understandable that taking tests can create a great deal of anxiety for many students. Even students who know they have learned the required material find their minds going blank as they stare at the test booklet. One easy way to overcome that anxiety is to prepare mentally for the test. Here are a few simple techniques.

Do not procrastinate

Study the material for the test when it becomes available, and continue to review the material until the test day. By waiting until the last minute and trying to cram for the test the night before, you actually increase anxiety. This leads to an increase in negative self-talk. Telling yourself "I can't learn this. I am going to fail" is a pretty sure indication that you are right. At best, your performance on the test will not be as strong if you have procrastinated instead of studying.

Positive self-talk.

Positive self-talk drowns out negative self-talk and to increases your confidence level. Whenever you begin feeling overwhelmed or anxious about the test, remind yourself that you have studied enough, you know the material and that you will pass the test. Both negative and positive self-talk are really just your fantasy, so why not choose to be a winner?

Do not compare yourself to others.

Do not compare yourself to other students. Instead, focus on your strengths and weaknesses and prepare accordingly. Regardless of how others perform, your performance is the only one that matters to your grade. Comparing yourself to others increases your anxiety and negative self-talk before the test.

Visualize.

Make a mental image of yourself taking the test. You know

the answers and feel relaxed. Visualize doing well on the test and having no problems with the material. Visualizations can increase your confidence and decrease the anxiety you might otherwise feel before the test. Instead of thinking of this as a test, see it as an opportunity to demonstrate what you have learned!

Avoid negativity.

Worry is contagious and viral - once it gets started it builds on itself. Cut it off before it gets to be a problem. Even if you are relaxed and confident, being around anxious, worried classmates might cause you to start feeling anxious. Before the test, tune out the fears of classmates. Feeling anxious and worried before an exam is normal, and every student experiences those feelings at some point. But you cannot allow these feelings to interfere with your ability to perform well. Practicing mental preparation techniques and remembering that the test is not the only measure of your academic performance will ease your anxiety and ensure that you perform at your best.

How to Take a Test

EVERYONE KNOWS THAT TAKING AN EXAM IS STRESSFUL, BUT IT DOES NOT HAVE TO BE THAT BAD! There are a few simple things that you can do to increase your score on any type of test. Take a look at these tips and consider how you can incorporate them into your study time.

Reading the Instructions

This is the most basic point, but one that, surprisingly, many students ignore and it costs big time! Since reading the instructions is one of the most common, and 100% preventable mistakes, we have a whole section just on reading instructions.

Pay close attention to the sample questions. Almost all standardized tests offer sample questions, paired with their correct solutions. Go through these to make sure that you understand what they mean and how they arrived at the correct answer. Do not be afraid to ask the test supervisor for help with a sample that confuses you, or instructions that you are unsure of.

Tips for Reading the Question

We could write pages and pages of tips just on reading the test questions. Here are a few that will help you the most.

- **Think first.** Before you look at the answer, read and think about the question. It is best to try to come up with the correct answer before you look at the options. This way, when the test-writer tries to trick you with a close answer, you will not fall for it.

- **Make it true or false.** If a question confuses you, then look at each answer option and think of it as a "true" "false" question. Select the one that seems most likely to be "true."

• **Mark the Question.** For some reason, a lot of test-takers are afraid to mark up their test booklet. Unless you are specifically told not to mark in the booklet, you should feel free to use it to your advantage.

• **Circle Key Words.** As you are reading the question, underline or circle key words. This helps you to focus on the most critical information needed to solve the problem. For example, if the question said, "Which of these is not a synonym for huge?" You might circle "not," "synonym" and "huge." That clears away the clutter and lets you focus on what is important.

• **Always underline these words:** all, none, always, never, most, best, true, false and except.

• **Eliminate.** Elimination is the best strategy for multiple choice answers *and* questions. If you are confused by lengthy questions, cross out anything that you think is irrelevant, obviously wrong, or information that you think is offered to distract you.

• **Do not try to read between the lines.** Usually, questions are written to be straightforward, with no deep, underlying meaning. Generally, the simple answer really is the correct answer. Do not over-analyze!

How to Take a Test - The Basics

Some sections of the test are designed to assess your ability to quickly grab the necessary information; this type of exam makes speed a priority. Others are more concerned with your depth of knowledge, and how accurate it is. When you start a new section of the test, look it over to determine whether the test is for speed or accuracy. If the test is for speed (a lot of questions and a short time), your strategy is clear; answer as many questions as quickly as possible.

The MELAB does NOT penalize for wrong answers, so if all else fails, guess and make sure you answer every question.

Make time your friend

Budget your time from the beginning until you are finished, and stick to it! The amount of time you are permitted for each portion of the test will almost certainly be included in the instructions.

Easy does it

One smart way to tackle a test is to locate the easy questions and answer those first. This is a time-tested strategy that never fails, because it saves you a lot of unnecessary anxiety. First, read the question and decide if you can answer it in less than a minute. If so, complete the question and go to the next one. If not, skip it for now and continue to the next question. By the time you have completed the first pass through this section of the exam, you will have answered a good number of questions. Not only does it boost your confidence, relieve anxiety and kick your memory up a notch, you will know exactly how many questions remain and can allot the rest of your time accordingly. Think of doing the easy questions first as a warm-up!

Do not watch your watch

At best, taking an important exam is an uncomfortable situation. If you are like most people, you might be tempted to subconsciously distract yourself from the task at hand. One of the most common ways to do so is by becoming obsessed with your watch or the wall clock. Do not watch your watch! Take it off and place it on the top corner of your desk, far enough away that you will not be tempted to look at it every two minutes. Better still, turn the watch face away from you.

That way, every time you try to sneak a peek, you will be reminded to refocus your attention to the task at hand. Give yourself permission to check your watch or the wall clock after you complete each section. Focus on answering the questions, not on how many minutes have elapsed since you last looked at it.

Divide and conquer

What should you do when you come across a question that is so complicated you may not even be certain what is being asked? As we have suggested, the first time through, skip the question. At some point, you will need to return to it and get it under control. The best way to handle questions that leave you feeling so anxious you can hardly think is by breaking them into manageable pieces. Solving smaller bits is always easier. For complicated questions, divide them into bite-sized pieces and solve these smaller sets separately. Once you understand what the reduced sections are really saying, it will be much easier to put them together and get a handle on the bigger question. This may not work with every question - see below for how to deal with questions you cannot break down.

Reason your way through the toughest questions

If you find that a question is so dense you can't figure out how to break it into smaller pieces, there are a few strategies that might help. First, read the question again and look for hints. Can you re-word the question in one or more different ways? This may give you clues. Look for words that can function as either verbs or nouns, and try to figure out what the questions is asking from the sentence structure. Remember that many nouns in English have several different meanings. While some of those meanings might be related, sometimes they are completely distinct. If reading the sentence one way does not make sense, consider a different definition or meaning for a key word.

The truth is, it is not always necessary to understand a question to arrive at a correct answer! The most successful strategy for multiple choice is Elimination. Frequently, at least one answer is clearly wrong and can be crossed off the list of possible correct answers. Next, look at the remaining answers and eliminate any that are only partially true. You may still have to flat-out guess from time to time, but using the process of elimination will help you make your way to the correct answer more often than not - even when you don't know what the question means!

Do not leave early

Use all the time allotted to you, even if you can't wait to get out of the testing room. Instead, once you have finished, spend the remaining time reviewing your answers. Go back to those questions that were most difficult for you and review your response. Another good way to use this time is to return to multiple-choice questions in which you filled in a bubble. Do a spot check, reviewing every fifth or sixth question to make sure your answer coincides with the bubble you filled in. This is a great way to catch yourself if you made a mistake, skipped a bubble and therefore put all your answers in the wrong bubbles!

Become a super sleuth and look for careless errors. Look for questions that have double negatives or other odd phrasing; they might be an attempt to throw you off. Careless errors on your part might be the result of skimming a question and missing a key word. Words such as "always," "never," "sometimes," "rarely" and the like can give a strong indication of the answer the question is really seeking. Don't throw away points by being careless!

Just as you budgeted time at the beginning of the test to allow for easy and more difficult questions, be sure to budget sufficient time to review your answers. On essay questions and math questions where you are required to show your work, check your writing to make sure it is legible.

Math questions can be especially tricky. The best way to double check math questions is by figuring the answer using a different method, if possible.

Here is another terrific tip. It is likely that no matter how hard you try, you will have a handful of questions you just are not sure of. Keep them in mind as you read through the rest of the test. If you can't answer a question, looking back over the test to find a different question that addresses the same topic might give you clues.

We know that taking the test has been stressful and you can hardly wait to escape. Just keep in mind that leaving before you double-check as much as possible can be a quick trip to disaster. Taking a few extra minutes can make the difference between getting a bad grade and a great one. Besides, there will be lots of time to relax and celebrate after the test is turned in.

In the Test Room – What you MUST do!

If you are like the rest of the world, there is almost nothing you would rather avoid than taking a test. Unfortunately, that is not an option if you want to pass. Rather than suffer, consider a few attitude adjustments that might turn the experience from a horrible one to...well, an interesting one! Take a look at these tips. Simply changing how you perceive the experience can change the experience itself.

You have to take the test - you can't change that. What you can change, and the only thing that you can change, is your attitude -so get a grip - you can do it!

Get in the mood

After weeks of studying, the big day has finally arrived. The worst thing you can do to yourself is arrive at the test site feeling frustrated, worried, and anxious. Keep a check on your emotional state. If your emotions are shaky before a test it can determine how well you do on the test. It is extremely important that you pump yourself up, believe in yourself, and use that confidence to get in the mood!

Don't fight reality

Students often resent tests, and with good reason. After all, many people do not test well, and they know the grade they end with does not accurately reflect their true knowledge. It is easy to feel resentful because tests classify students and create categories that just don't seem fair. Face it: Students who are great at rote memorization and not that good at actually analyzing material often score higher than those who might be more creative thinkers and balk at simply memorizing cold, hard facts. It may not be fair, but there it is anyway. Conformity is an asset on tests, and creativity is often a liability. There is no point in wasting time or energy being upset about this reality. Your first step is to accept the reality and get used to it. You will get higher marks when you realize tests do count and that you must give them your best effort. Think about your future and the career that is easier to achieve if you have consistently earned high grades. Avoid negative energy and focus on anything that lifts your enthusiasm and increases your motivation.

Get there early enough to relax

If you are wound up, tense, scared, anxious, or feeling rushed, it will cost you. Get to the exam room early and relax before you go in. This way, when the exam starts, you are comfortable and ready to apply yourself. Of course, you do not want to arrive so early that you are the only one there. That will not help you relax; it will only give you too much time to sit there, worry and get wound up all over again.

If you can, visit the room where you will be taking your exam a few days ahead of time. Having a visual image of the room can be surprisingly calming, because it takes away one of the big 'unknowns'. Not only that, but once you have visited, you know how to get there and will not be worried about getting lost. Furthermore, driving to the test site once lets you know how much time you need to allow for the trip. That means three potential stressors have been eliminated all at once.

Get it down on paper

One advantage of arriving early is that it allows you time to recreate notes. If you spend a lot of time worrying about whether you will be able to remember information like names, dates, places, and mathematical formulas, there is a solution for that. Unless the exam you are taking allows you to use your books and notes, (and very few do) you will have to rely on memory. Arriving early gives to time to tap into your memory and jot down key pieces of information you know that will be asked. Just make certain you are allowed to make notes once you are in the testing site; not all locations will permit it. Once you get your test, on a small piece of paper write down everything you are afraid you will forget. It will take a minute or two but by dumping your worries onto the page you have effectively eliminated a certain amount of anxiety and driven off the panic you feel.

Get comfortable in your chair

Here is a clever technique that releases physical stress and helps you get comfortable, even relaxed in your body. You will tense and hold each of your muscles for just a few seconds. The trick is, you must tense them hard for the technique to work. You might want to practice this technique a few times at home; you do not want an unfamiliar technique to add to your stress just before a test, after all! Once you are at the test site, this exercise can always be done in the rest room or another quiet location.

Start with the muscles in your face then work down your body. Tense, squeeze and hold the muscles for a moment or two. Notice the feel of every muscle as you go down your body. Scowl to tense your forehead, pull in your chin to tense your neck. Squeeze your shoulders down to tense your back. Pull in your stomach all the way back to your ribs, make your lower back tight then stretch your fingers. Tense your leg muscles and calves then stretch your feet and your toes. You should be as stiff as a board throughout your entire body.

Now relax your muscles in reverse starting with your toes. Notice how all the muscles feel as you relax them one by one.

Once you have released a muscle or set of muscles, allow them to remain relaxed as you proceed up your body. Focus on how you are feeling as all the tension leaves. Start breathing deeply when you get to your chest muscles. By the time you have found your chair, you will be so relaxed it will feel like bliss!

Fight distraction

A lucky few are able to focus deeply when taking an important examination, but most people are easily distracted, probably because they would rather be any place else! There are a number of things you can do to protect yourself from distraction.

Stay away from windows.

If you select a seat near a window you may end gazing out at the landscape instead of paying attention to the work at hand. Furthermore, any sign of human activity, from a single individual walking by to a couple having an argument or exchanging a kiss will draw your attention away from your important work. What goes on outside should not be allowed to distract you.

Choose a seat away from the aisle so you do not become distracted by people who leave early. People who leave the exam room early are often the ones who fail. Do not compare your time to theirs.

Of course, you love your friends; that's why they are your friends! In the test room, however, they should become complete strangers inside your mind. Forget they are there. The first step is to physically distance yourself from friends or classmates. That way, you will not be tempted to glance at them to see how they are doing, and there will be no chance of eye contact that could either distract you or even lead to an accusation of cheating. Furthermore, if they are feeling stressed because they did not spend the focused time studying that you did, their anxiety is less likely to permeate your hard-earned calm.

Of course, you will want to choose a seat where there is sufficient light. Nothing is worse than trying to take an important examination under flickering lights or dim bulbs.

Ask the instructor or exam proctor to close the door if there is a lot of noise outside. If the instructor or proctor is unable to do so, block out the noise as best you can. Do not let anything disturb you.

The PAX does not allow any personal items in the exam room. Eat protein, complex carbohydrates and a little fat to keep you feeling full and to supercharge your energy. Nothing is worse than a sudden drop in blood sugar during an exam.

Do not allow yourself to become distracted by being too cold or hot. Regardless of the weather outside, carry a sweater, scarf or jacket if the air conditioning at the test site is set too high, or the heat set too low. By the same token, dress in layers so that you are prepared for a range of temperatures.

Watch Caffeine

Drinking a gallon of coffee or gulping a few energy drinks might seem like a great idea, but it is, in fact, a very bad one. Caffeine, pep pills or other artificial sources of energy are more likely to leave you feeling rushed and ragged. Your brain might be clicking along, all right, but chances are good it is not clicking along on the right track! Furthermore, drinking lots of coffee or energy drinks will mean frequent trips to the rest room. This will cut into the time you should be spending answering questions and is a distraction in itself, since each time you need to leave the room you lose focus. Pep pills will only make it harder for you to think straight when solving complicated problems on the exam.

At the same time, if anxiety is your problem try to find ways around using tranquilizers during test-taking time. Even medically prescribed anti-anxiety medication can make you less alert and even decrease your motivation. Being motivated is what you need to get you through an exam. If your anxiety is so bad that it threatens to interfere with your ability to take an exam, speak to your doctor and ask for documentation. Many testing sites will allow non-distracting test rooms, extended testing time and other accommodations as long as a doctor's note that explains the situation is made available.

Keep Breathing

It might not make a lot of sense, but when people become anxious, tense, or scared, their breathing becomes shallow and, in some cases, they stop breathing all together! Pay attention to your emotions, and when you are feeling worried, focus on your breathing. Take a moment to remind yourself to breathe deeply and regularly. Drawing in steady, deep breaths energizes the body. When you continue to breathe deeply you will notice you exhale all the tension.

It is a smart idea to rehearse breathing at home. With continued practice of this relaxation technique, you will begin to know the muscles that tense up under pressure. Call these your "signal muscles." These are the ones that will speak to you first, begging you to relax. Take the time to listen to those muscles and do as they ask. With just a little breathing practice, you will get into the habit of checking yourself regularly and when you realize you are tense, relaxation will become second nature.

Avoid Anxiety Before a Test

Manage your time effectively

This is a key to your success! You need blocks of uninterrupted time to study all the pertinent material. Creating and maintaining a schedule will help keep you on track, and will remind family members and friends that you are not available. Under no circumstances should you change your blocks of study time to accommodate someone else, or cancel a study session to do something more fun. Do not interfere with your study time for any reason!

Relax

Use whatever works best for you to relieve stress. Some folks like a good, calming stretch with yoga, others find expressing themselves through journaling to be useful. Some hit the floor for a series of crunches or planks, and still others take a slow stroll around the garden. Integrate a little relaxation time into your schedule, and treat that time, too, as sacred.

Eat healthy

Instead of reaching for the chips and chocolate, fresh fruits and vegetables are not only yummy but offer nutritional benefits that help to relieve stress. Some foods accelerate stress instead of reducing it and should be avoided. Foods that add to higher anxiety include artificial sweeteners, candy and other sugary foods, carbonated sodas, chips, chocolate, eggs, fried foods, junk foods, processed foods, red meat, and other foods containing preservatives or heavy spices. Instead, eat a bowl of berries and some yogurt!

Get plenty of ZZZZZZZs

Do not cram or try to do an all-nighter. If you created a study schedule at the beginning, and if you have stuck with that schedule, have confidence! Staying up too late trying to cram in last-minute bits of information is going to leave you exhausted the next day. Besides, whatever new information you cram in will only displace all the important ideas you've spent weeks learning. Remember: You need to be alert and fully functional the day of the exam

Have confidence in yourself!

Everyone experiences some anxiety when taking a test, but exhibiting a positive attitude banishes anxiety and fills you with the knowledge you really do know what you need to know. This is your opportunity to show how well prepared you are. Go for it!

Be sure to take everything you need

Depending on the exam, you may be allowed to have a pen or pencil, calculator, dictionary or scratch paper with you. Have these gathered together along with your entrance paperwork and identification so that you are sure you have everything that is needed.

Do not chitchat with friends

Let your friends know ahead of time that it is not anything personal, but you are going to ignore them in the test room! You need to find a seat away from doors and windows, one that has good lighting, and get comfortable. If other students are worried their anxiety could be detrimental to you; of course, you do not have to tell your friends that. If you are afraid they will be offended, tell them you are protecting them from your anxiety!

Common Test-Taking Mistakes

Taking a test is not much fun at best. When you take a test and make a stupid mistake that negatively affects your grade, it is natural to be very upset, especially when it is something that could have been easily avoided. So what are some of the common mistakes that are made on tests?

Do not fail to put your name on the test

How could you possibly forget to put your name on a test? You would be amazed at how often that happens. Very often, tests without names are thrown out immediately, resulting in a failing grade.

Marking the wrong multiple-choice answer

It is important to work at a steady pace, but that does not mean bolting through the questions. Be sure the answer you are marking is the one you mean to. If the bubble you need to fill in or the answer you need to circle is 'C', do not allow yourself to get distracted and select 'B' instead.

Answering a question twice

Some multiple-choice test questions have two very similar answers. If you are in too much of a hurry, you might select them both. Remember that only one answer is correct, so if you choose more than one, you have automatically failed that question.

Mishandling a difficult question

We recommend skipping difficult questions and returning to them later, but beware! First, be certain that you do return to the question. Circling the entire passage or placing a large question mark beside it will help you spot it when you are reviewing your test. Secondly, if you are not careful to skip the question, you can mess yourself up badly. Imagine that a question is too difficult and you decide to save it for later. You read the next question, which you know the answer to, and you fill in that answer. You continue to the end of the test then return to the difficult question only to discover you didn't actually skip it! Instead, you inserted the answer to the following question in the spot reserved for the harder one, thus throwing off the remainder of your test!

Incorrectly Transferring an answer from scratch paper

This can happen easily if you are trying to hurry! Double check any answer you have figured out on scratch paper, and make sure what you have written on the test itself is an exact match!

Thinking too much

Oftentimes, your first thought is your best thought. If you worry yourself into insecurity, your self-doubts can trick you into choosing an incorrect answer when your first impulse was the right one!

CONCLUSION

CONGRATULATIONS! You have made it this far because you have applied yourself diligently to practicing for the exam and no doubt improved your potential score considerably! Getting into a good school is a huge step in a journey that might be challenging at times but will be many times more rewarding and fulfilling. That is why being prepared is so important.

Study then Practice and then Succeed!

Good Luck!

THANKS!

I f you enjoyed this book and would like to order additional copies for yourself or for friends, please check with your local bookstore, favorite online bookseller or visit www.test-preparation.ca and place your order directly with the publisher.

Feedback to the author may be sent by email to feedback@test-preparation.ca

ENDNOTES

[1] The Immune System. In *Wikipedia*. Retrieved Feb 14, 2009, from http://en.wikipedia.org/wiki/Immune_system.

[2] White Blood Cell. In *Wikipedia*. Retrieved Feb 14, 2009, from http://en.wikipedia.org/wiki/White_blood_cell.

[3] Thunderstorm. In *Wikipedia*. Retrieved Feb 14, 2009, from http://en.wikipedia.org/wiki/Thunderstorm/

[4] *Wiktionary*. Retrieved Feb 14, 2009, from http://http://en.wiktionary.org/wiki/.

[5] Volcano. *Wikipedia*. Retrieved May 9, 2012, from http://en.wikipedia.org/wiki/Volcano.

[6] Rabbit. *Wikipedia*. Retrieved May 9, 2012, from http://en.wikipedia.org/wiki/Rabbits

[7] Human Encyclopedia. Retrieved May 9, 2012, from http://www.facebook.com/pages/Human-Encyclopedia/243885452309916

[8] Infectious Disease. In *Wikipedia*. Retrieved Feb 14, 2009, from http://en.wikipedia.org/wiki/Infectious_disease.

[9] Virus. In *Wikipedia*. Retrieved Feb 14, 2009, from http://en.wikipedia.org/wiki/Virus.

[10] Outline of Meteorology. In *Wikipedia*. Retrieved Feb 14, 2009, from http://en.wikipedia.org/wiki/Outline_of_meteorology.

[11] Butterfly. In *Wikipedia*. Retrieved Feb 14, 2009, from http://http://en.wikipedia.org/wiki/Butterfly.

[12] United States Navy SEALs. In *Wikipedia*. Retrieved Feb 14, 2009, from http://en.wikipedia.org/wiki/United_States_Navy_SEALs.

[13] Fox. In *Wikipedia*. Retrieved May 9, 2012, from http://

en.wikipedia.org/wiki/Fox.

[14] Carroll, Lewis. *Alice in Wonderland*. Chapter 11. http://www.gutenberg.org/files/11/11-h/11-h.htm#2HCH0011.

[15] Respiratory System. In *Wikipedia*. Retrieved Feb 14, 2009, from
http://en.wikipedia.org/wiki/Respiratory_system.

[16] Mythology. In *Wikipedia*. Retrieved Feb 14, 2009, from
http://en.wikipedia.org/wiki/Mythology.

[17] Insects. In *Wikipedia*. Retrieved Feb 14, 2009, from
http://en.wikipedia.org/wiki/Insect.

[18] Tree. In *Wikipedia*. Retrieved Feb 14, 2009, from
http://en.wikipedia.org/wiki/Tree.

[19] Kipling, Rudyard. *The Jungle Book*. http://www.gutenberg.org/files/236/236-h/236-h.htm#2H_4_0011.

[20] Blood. In *Wikipedia*. Retrieved May 9, 2012, from http://en.wikipedia.org/wiki/Blood.

[21] Human Skeleton. In *Wikipedia*. Retrieved May 9, 2012, from en.wikipedia.org/wiki/Human_skeleton.

[22] Clouds. In *Wikipedia*. Retrieved May 9, 2012, from en.wikipedia.org/wiki/Cloud.

[23] Gardening. In *Wikipedia*. Retrieved May 9, 2012, From en.wikipedia.org/wiki/Gardening.

[24] Coral Reef. In *Wikipedia*. Retrieved May 9, 2012, from en.wikipedia.org/wiki/Coral_reef

CPSIA information can be obtained
at www.ICGtesting.com
Printed in the USA
LVOW13s0051150917

548754LV00014B/351/P